CAN THESE BONES LIVE?

CAN THESE BONES LIVE?

The Failure of Church Renewal

Robert S. Lecky and H. Elliott Wright
with a Foreword by Rosemary Ruether

SHEED AND WARD : NEW YORK

For B. J. Stiles and Vanderbilt Divinity School

. . . and set me down in the midst of the valley; it was full of bones. And he led me round among them; and behold, there were very many upon the valley; and lo, they were very dry. And he said to me, "Son of man, can these bones live?" And I answered, "O Lord God, thou knowest."

Ezek. 37:1a-3

Contents

Foreword and Counterpoint

Then the nations that are left round about you
shall know that I, the Lord, have rebuilt the
ruined places, and replanted that which was
desolate; I, the Lord, have spoken, and I will
do it. (Ezek. 36:36)

Why should a book on church renewal start with the assumption that the topic is a boring one? Surely the reason is that church renewal is typically viewed as an ingrown, parochial topic, an ecclesiastical navel-gazing. From this perspective the topic can only evoke bored *déjà vu* and a tacit consent beforehand that "these bones cannot live." To give some life to these bones we must start, not from institutional introspection, but from theological vision, and lay again upon the community the demand to live out of that vision as its mandate.

In its roots and original vision Christianity is a messianic movement. This statement should hardly be startling since the very word Christian means simply "messianist." What Christians meant when they said "Jesus is the Christ" was that, in the events surrounding the life and death of Jesus the Nazarene, the "turn of the ages" had begun. This was the turn of the ages expected as the final day of world judgment and re-creation predicted by the prophets and apocalypticists of Israel. The turn of the ages meant the final cosmic "revolution," the end of the world with its political systems, its oppression of body, mind and spirit. It would inaugurate the new age of the resurrection of the dead when men live a transfigured and free life out beyond this historical bondage.

This pattern of thought is perhaps less strange to us today than it was in the heyday of liberalism. It has been the basis of a continuous rebirth of the revolutionary tradition in religious and later in socio-economic language down to our own time. It is in this sense that Christians, although not the Constantinian church, can claim to be founders and heirs of the revolutionary tradition in the West. They can claim this revolutionary tradition in its most radical form, encompassing not merely change in environment or institutions, but a change in the very nature and character of man himself, tending toward the "New Adam" who must be born out of the death of historical man. Indeed all revolutionary thought, no matter how "secular" its language, must envision an inner transformation of man himself as the basis of the new world that will rise on the other side of the revolution. The failure to create the "new Man" is the key to the failure of every revolution short of the ultimate revolution.

The Christian is the vanguard of the most profound revolutionary tradition, one which cannot compromise with any partial revolution that brings in merely altered institutions, better socio-economic arrangements, improved technology and the like. These may be a part of the ultimate revolution, but the Christian must press on through and beyond these partial revolutions to the final transformation of the nature of man and the renovation of the universe. This is what makes the Christian revolutionary the continual "New Left" out beyond every partisan leftism which may make itself into a new establishment, whether ecclesial or political.

The church in its true nature cannot be equated with any institutional party, but must be understood as the ever-reborn revolutionary brotherhood, whose continuity is not a continuity of organization, but a continuity of inner principle of life. This is the authentic apostolic succession, in contrast to the secondary apostolic successions of bishops or party chairmen. It follows that one does not find where the church is by consulting the local paper for lists of church organizations, or going to the local chancery to find one's geographical parish or looking for buildings with a peculiar form of architecture. One finds where the church is by assessing the signs of the times and testing the existing historical conditions to discover where the struggle against dehumanization and falsehood and for truth and real life is taking place. That is where the Holy Spirit is at work and that is where the church is. The church is the brotherhood of the new world, the community of the resurrection. It is to be found in and as that community at the heart of the struggle for the salvation of man in any era. The church is where the Spirit is. This is not a new principle; it is the oldest principle of ecclesiology.

How does one gather the church? The first principle that we must recognize is the partiality and relativity of all of our gatherings of the church. Ultimately no man gathers the church; only the Holy Spirit gathers the church. The church is truly gathered at the points where the renewal of the world is taking place. Those who carry a great load of institutional baggage about this word "church" should be asked to look to where this renewal is really taking place and then ask how their tradition and institution can plug into it there. For most of us this means relating to possibilities of rebirth wherever one happens to be. Sometimes this means getting up and moving out to "a far country" but, for most of us, that journey is simply to turn around where we are.

The church as the revolutionary brotherhood faces over against the institutional powers and principalities of this world, including that part of the power structure of this world which calls itself "church." If we are especially concerned with renewing this particular institution, it is only as a part —perhaps no more crucial part than any other—of the renewal of the world. The final conclusion of this revolution is not to bring the world into the historical church, but to bring the world, including all the churches of the world, into the Kingdom of God. The messianic brotherhood is spirit-born and is not an institutionally gathered and defined community. It is found in relation to all institutions and structures of the world insofar as there is a tension of death and rebirth going on within them.

The basic stance of the messianic brotherhood toward every institution is dialectical. It simultaneously defines itself over against the egoistic and self-perpetuating life principle of that institution, and, at the same time, continues to faithfully relate to and confront that institution in order to overthrow it from within. In so doing, it seeks to open up the possibility of a rebirth in freedom that appears when the old world of institutional self-perpetuation is brought to the cross. The messianic brotherhood acts as the perpetual revolutionary force within and against every worldly power structure: ecclesiastical, political or social. Its task is to remain within this dialectic in each situation and in each historical period in which it finds itself, until the disparity between man's existence and his essence, that is to say, the disparity between the human and the divine, earth and heaven is finally overcome. This is the state of being for which Jesus admonished us to pray to Our Heavenly Father: "Thy Kingdom Come (that is to say), Thy will be done *on earth*, as it is in Heaven."

Rosemary Raford Ruether

Introduction / Another Book on Church Renewal?

A decade ago, in the period of expanding civil rights activities, a seminary professor greeted a class: "This has been a wonderful day. I signed another petition and everyone here knows how important that is. Petitions make the world go round. I was opening my office door this morning when I saw a colleague walking down the hall. 'Thank you, God,' I said, 'here comes another petition.'"

The professor's weariness with "another petition" could well be a reader's reaction to "another book" on church renewal. They are plentiful. Another anything calling for church renewal or describing, for didactic purposes, updating church experiences would be a non-contribution to the contemporary scene, religious or secular. Abundantly, the point has been made that traditional Christian forms are in trouble. Written documentaries on attempts to extricate the church from dilemma are overly plentiful. After all, renewal became during the late 1950's and early 1960's the charge of the future for most major churches. Another clamorous extolling or describing is useless.

It is pertinent, however, to wonder what has happened to church renewal. Much of its early sixties zing has been lost, though its language increasingly dominates the ecclesiastical sphere. Very little in the enormous literature of renewal raises questions about what the church thinks renewal really is or where it is going.

This book is an attempt to deal with ramifications of a blunt question put by Carlyle Marney, the famed North Carolina preacher. "Renew what?" he asked in a sermon in New York's Riverside Church.

The question has been asked before, usually by those of a conservative inclination who think no changes are needed in Christianity except possibly response to the demand "face to the rear." Dr. Marney made a request for clarity. His was no rhetorical introduction to praise of the status quo or for retrogression. These chapters share his concern. They originated from the desire to delineate with some degree of sharpness the shape of the contemporary church's involvements. If observations are intertwined with opinions, it is because the authors believe there is no value in sterile, unevaluative discourses on religion.

Dr. Marney's "renew what?" has been dealt with only superficially among renewal's enthusiastic propounders. This factor suggests that church updating as generic occurrence is unclear about its aims and intentions. Few have stood a moment and inquired, "What is going on here?"

When the looking stance is taken—and it is sinfully comfortable to jump off the going bandwagon for a time—the field of church renewal takes on the appearance of the valley of bones in which Ezekiel found himself. It is no proud ship self-assuredly running before the breath of God's blowing.

Agreement among churchmen that change is necessary is widespread enough to justify metaphorical application of Ezekiel's vision to church renewal: bonelike. Bones in the prophet's experience represent life and lifelessness. Renewal as commonly viewed is life-giving. Is it? As Ezekiel found the valley, renewal may be more accurately seen as bits and pieces not yet fitted together. It may be only the movement of bones.

The suspicion sneaks in that, in trying to bring forth a whole, healthy entity with flesh and sinew, many advocates have allowed renewal *qua* renewal to become substance as well as a church survival program Rudolf Bultmann and others say one of the earliest developments in Christianity was that in which the proclaimer, Jesus, became the proclaimed, Jesus Christ. As new savior of an imperiled church, renewal may well be on the way to the same deification. God's ability to work his will as he chooses is not in doubt. It is dangerous, on the other hand, to put too much trust in a savior who (or which) has not died and been given undying life by divine volition.

This book agrees with Colin Morris, the former president of the United Church of Zambia, that it is both "futile and callow" to expect formulas for renewal to take the place of a zealous humanism in which theology reflects upon the actions of the "people of God" but seeks not to initiate that action.[1] The possibility of alternatives to the present renewal valley is, therefore, opened up. Whether the church is renewed or lives as unresuscitated institutions becomes a matter secondary to new life for humanity. Maybe humanity alive is, in final analysis, the church anyway.

The authors bear responsibility for ideas and opinions expressed, but many persons and organizations lent assistance in the months spent writing this book. Thanks is due to *Christianity and Crisis* magazine for directly and indirectly providing resource material and contacts. Several scores of the well and lesser known from the modern religious scene generously gave their time in helpful conversation. Their insights, warnings and encouragements are appreciated. Frank

White, of the National Council of Churches' Division of Christian Life and Mission, merits special mention for counsel and for sharing a wealth of data.

Words of thanks could not be completed without tribute to our wives, Joan Lecky and Juanita Wright, for patience, incentive and love. In a professional but willing capacity, Juanita typed the manuscript. More importantly, she labored to make style consistent and to keep boss and husband from completely falling off the end of ideological limbs.

May Day, 1969

Notes

[1] Colin Morris, *Include Me Out!* (Nashville: Abingdon Press, 1968), p. 99.

CAN THESE BONES LIVE?

PART ONE / *Coming From*

1 / Renewal Fever

. . . there was a noise, and behold, a rattling; and the bones came together, bone to its bone (Ezek. 37:7).

The Christian church as institutions is not dead, but it wants to be yet more alive. Meet the vitalizer: renewal. Virtually defying definition, renewal is a catch-all phenomenon signifying what all non-stand-pat and some tradition-clutching churchmen are doing and thinking in an age which, from a conservative view, is transition, but which, from a radical perspective, may open onto a churchless era. Renewal is Christianity's Barbara Graham-like plea to judge, jury, executioner and public: "I want to live" some more, beyond tomorrow.

Suggestion of a church not already quite dead, of course, goes against the fringes of the avant-garde and the camp followers blowing their minds on ecclesiastical obituaries. A "death-of-the-church" movement may be a further indication that religion is also subject to Freud's claim that humans have a death urge, the "death-of-God" being the first assault.

The dead church talk, actually, is a journalistic phenomenon, taking over when "death-of-God" faded. In the last five years, theology and journalism have become rather indistinguishable. Place exists for church and religion in the press. It would seem that the better relationship would be one of dialogue instead of mutual displacement.

5

A dead institutional church is no more the case because of popularization of the notion than deity's demise was irrefutable after *Time* magazine ran a black cover in 1967. Theology's age-old anti-Thomistic claim that the existence of God cannot be proved applies equally to efforts to disprove. They are empty. To say that church is dead is not the same as the claim that God is dead, except in one respect.

All doctrines of the church posit two dimensions: visible and invisible, particular and universal, militant and triumphant. The invisible-universal-triumphant church fits into the same category with God; it is not available for litmus paper tests. But the visible-particular-militant church has institutional force. Most of the dead church tomes avoid the first dimensions—abstract doctrine is basically unjournalistic —so that it is the church with shape which is declared dead.

In terms of ability to steer persons toward meaning, maturity and kindliness, the church may have been effectively dead for years. Institutionally, however, it lives. By definition an institution is organization, structure; to wit, the church. A genuine prophet might know for certain that Christianity's structures are doomed. The church neither knows nor accepts any such thing. It intends to live, and never mind the comfortable words about "being of God . . . preserved to the end of time." The church has renewal. Selah!

If and when the church vanishes or is killed, church renewal will accompany it. Renewalists make a point of noting how the surge to update, change and revitalize the church and the ideas the church propels through history came from within. That is true. Ignored is the fact that renewal must be tended as carefully as the traditionalism it is meant to replace or interpret. Renewal, these pages assert, is neither harbinger or task-master of Christianity. It is the church's ward, a child whose birth brought celebration to dusty mansions, an infant whom the church has no intention of allowing to grow to independent maturity.

This conclusion is reached because renewal shares the neuroses of its parent: perplexity, unsurefootedness, craftiness and too much concern with survival. Moreover, there is yet no assurance that a hefty segment of the church will not decide to smother renewal while the nurses are on a field trip. It could well be killed by conservative counterreaction. Christopher Derrick, a conservative British Roman Catholic layman and author, after an early 1969 speaking tour throughout the United States, said that he found strong sentiment against constant changes in the church. Parallel sentiment exists in Protestantism. Brake-pumping by majority vote does not make it good nor justify backtracking, but it does intimate that persons may have misunderstood developments. Ignorance as well as villainy can build walls which halt.

More likely, if the church and its renewing die, they will fizzle out because they cannot withstand the fatigue and anxiety produced by their own floundering and inability to know what they are. The same week that Derrick reported on his observations about U.S. Catholicism, *The Christian Century* published thoughts about Protestantism's condition.[1] Theological exhaustion, ecumenical doldrums, parish bafflement and devotional emptiness were the labels used. A branch of Christianity in such a state of health bears scanty witness to over a decade of renewing fervor.

An overview of renewal encompasses manifold complexity, a scene of confusion, competition, replays, self-righteousness and, maybe, paralysis, as well as strides toward experimentation, relevance, innovations, ecumenical cooperation and church activism All are thoroughly mixed. Development in the future of two kinds of churches—leaving aside confessional names—is possible, one devoted to the status quo and the other pressing in new directions. For the time being there is only one kind of church among the major communions, the church rushing to renew.

Life Is Not Health

To say that the institutional church is not dead is not to say it is the picture of health. The matter at hand is what *is*. What *ought* to be is another story. Nothing institutional is factually dead which can mass as many people for meetings and spend as much money as can the modern churches, individually and collectively.

Howls of poverty have recently been heard—the smaller the percentage of church membership growth in relation to the overall population, the louder the howl. Some local and national churches have cut budgets. Granting that the per capita constituent increases were less than one per cent a year in the late 1960's, U.S. membership is enormously high, at least half the population, even when 12 percentage points are subtracted as error margin in the 1969 National Council of Churches' report. Honor requires that slice from the 62 per cent reported, since how a 1968 church membership percentage increase over the year before can be figured from statistics extending from 1939 to 1967 remains a mystery.

The significance of any Gallup Poll is open to question; still it is interesting to note that the survey agency said 98 per cent of Americans believed in God in 1968 but only 43 per cent went to church. One implication is that religion and church are not synonymous. A spiffy article in the March 1969 *Ladies Home Journal* suggested that even women are deciding "you can't find God in church anymore." In documenting the so-called "spiritual crisis," however, only 1,000 women were questioned, certainly not a very representative numerical proportion of female America. Gallup bolstered the claim: only 48 percent of women attended church in 1968 as compared to 55 percent in 1958.

Nonetheless, a 48 percent attendance of women at church services and a 43 percent overall participation is high. The Archbishop of Canterbury or the Cardinal of Paris might pray to be so fortunate. Even if the U.S. church dwindle continues at the same rate Gallup discovered in the previous decade, it would take considerable years for the church to be memberless. Were the percentage to double, it would still take more years for the church to die than some social prophets allow a habitable earth, unless the problems of hunger, war, pollution and overpopulation are solved.

Financially, the church is as secure as Wall Street, (before and after the economic demands of the Black Manifesto). The hierarchical denominations could live on and on merely from the sale of property abandoned as membership dropped. Complete and accurate information on the churches' wealth in the U.S., only one country, is perennially unavailable. As D. B. Robertston stated in *Should Churches Be Taxed?*, many churches honestly say they have no idea of total assets.[2] Any figures—on stock and real estate value, contributions and endowment—are estimates, estimates which soar into the billions. A 1968 American Association of Fund-Raising Council, Inc. report, covering the preceding 12 months said 46.9 per cent of the $14,569,000,000 given for philanthropic causes went to religion. A conservative estimate of the Vatican's stock holdings, according to Nino Lo Bello, a newsman who researched for ten years, is $5 billion.[3] Figures given in the Italian Parliment have ranged considerably lower, and many disagree with Lo Bello's claim that the Vatican is the largest financial power in the world. Whatever the total, it is substantial.

Robertson summed up: "Whatever the difficulties in determining the extent of church wealth, it is obvious that it is
great and that it is growing rapidly."[4] He also recalled Eugene
Carson Blake, now general secretary of the World Council
of Churches, remarking in 1959 that "it is not unreasonable
to prophesy that with reasonably prudent management, the
churches ought to be able to control the whole economy of
the nation within the predictable future."[5] How long ahead
a predictable future is or how prudent church managers are,
Dr. Blake failed to prophesy.

Should a financial crisis arise, churches have the same option open to businesses: merger for the sake of larger economic bases. Perhaps smaller church units have already seen
the advantages. It could not have been altogether for love of
John Wesley that the less than a million-member Evangelical
United Brethren denomination permitted itself in 1968
to be fed into the yawning mouth of its enormous and top-
heavy Methodist sister. Rumors were that impending EUB
membership-financial problems flowed away as easily as identity, once merged.

Rattlings of New Life

Despite some statistical tremors and financial ponderings, and
especially despite a rash of church-burying journalism, the
institutional church exists, a non-wished-away reality To
their credit churchmen of many vintages have not been and
are not willing that church merely exist. Countless are genuinely concerned that message and structure be relevant to
denizens of the 20th century world, supportive of meaningful
lives, reassuring in turbulence and wise in leadership. That
renewal appears to be primarily the labor of preserving the
church is not necessarily intentional.

Retrospectively, the linking of the concept "church" and the renewal spirit may have been an unfortunate turn of events. "Church" is primarily an institutional term with heavy traditional overtones. Church, whether Catholic, Orthodox or Protestant, referred to one of the two spheres of power in the long centuries of Christendom, now by common agreement a bygone. When, with objective justification, J. C. Hoekendijk pleaded for the realization that Christendom was literally gone, and by direct implication Teilhard de Chardin earlier did the same, perhaps the term "church" should have been dropped. Better may have been something similar to Karl Rahner's phrase "the future reality of the Christian life."[6] Not, of course, that Rahner would approve of dispensing with "church," or even "Christendom" in certain respects.

Rahner touched on a plausible, open Christian faith, unfettered by worn out ecclesiastical language, when he wrote of the situation of a future Catholic: "At that future date there will be Christian or Catholic communities all over the world, though not evenly distributed. Everywhere they will be a little flock, because mankind grows quicker than Christendom and because men will not be Christians by custom or tradition, through institutions and history, or because of the homogeneity of a social milieu and public opinion, but . . . they will be Christians only because of their own act of faith attained in a difficult struggle and perpetually achieved anew."[7]

Definitely to be regretted are recent popular religion books —some strangely unstimulating before their fifth anniversaries—which speak of renewal as a necessity for church survival. And Harvey Cox lent a bit of confusion by referring to the church as "God's avant-garde."[8] He meant the avant-garde in a new regime of Christian proclamation, service and fellowship. His word was, nevertheless, packed with meanings provided by an old regime in need of renewal. When situations have really changed, renewed paraphernalia brought over from the old may be less relevant than insights of singular newness.

Should the future of the church depend upon a consensus description of renewal's impact and aims, there would be no future. The church has been learning for centuries that lack of consensus is frequently less disruptive than attempts to obtain agreement. Either out of wisdom or conditioning, therefore, renewal stands today as a major Christian preoccupation defying definition.

The number of active and dormant renewal concepts and examples abroad are enough to keep a computer blinking for days making a catalog. Under the rubric fall a potentially inexhaustible list. A sampling: modest liturgical innovations replacing "thee's" with "you's," and all-out ritual renovations placing bare dancing feet on marble altars; a Roman Pope praying alongside the Eastern Orthodox Ecumenical Patriarch, and intercommunion thrusts making pontiff and patriarch shudder; efforts to unite nine American Protestant denominations through a Consultation on Church Union, and local lay-led congregations which foreswear denominational affiliations; Vatican involvement in the course of economic development in poor nations, and papal rejection of a secularized priesthood working in the world to try filling empty parish churches; church-organized protests hurling invectives against corrupt political structures, and priests massing to ask ouster of an archbishop; the National Council of Churches fighting bigotry, and a black churchman walking out on the National Council because he saw it weak on antidiscrimination; denominations revising Christian education curriculum to weed out racism, and an Episcopal group burning new church literature for being too racist; Christian unity's trumpets louder than ever, along with increasing assertions that ecumenical house worship is expanding, and churches closing; social thrusts in all directions, and theology admitting it has trouble finding a course, and everybody wondering where the students have gone. The students used to be caught up in renewal. They have fled.

"Renewal's" Elusive Meaning

Is it surprising that few practitioners or theorists of renewal have tried a definition? Compilers of religious word books and encyclopedists leave the term alone. It appears in titles, tables of contents and talks but seldom in indices or summaries. "Renewal" has been applied to every structure, thought and motion directly or indirectly attachable to church. It is movement, process, a stirring of institutional bones and bodies, not dead but not quite alive enough to get up and go any place.

One of the first renewal books, Gibson Winter's *The Suburban Capitivity of the Churches* in 1961, spoke directly to the "focus,"—urban America in that case. Except for a few other well-conceptualized case studies, great quantities of renewal material is propositional, untried and theologically wishy-washy. This is particularly true of denominational study courses which take a soft sell approach to the nature of social conditions and to church responsibility. Take, for example, the *Crisis in America*[9] booklet emerging from the National Council's high-priority, low-budget program of the same name. The document qualifies as a study book since it was officially accepted as such by several denominations and eventually received Catholic and Jewish endorsement.

The preface commences by telling Americans—only shortly

earlier informed by a Presidential Commission that "white racism" was ruining the nation—that ". . . for the next several hundred years the city, not the frontier, will be the place of renewal, the symbol of challenge . . . the writers believe that the crisis of the cities is a troubling of the waters by the Holy Spirit, an effort by the body politic to throw off its disease, the birth pangs of a new day. We need to step into the waters with hope in order to be healed."[10]

But gently, gently must the National Council step, so many there are to be pleased. Must it not be noticed that it was after Watts and Orangeburg; Detroit and Selma; Newark and Clinton, Tennessee, that the National Council identified a "crisis in the nation" threatening to erupt in massive destruction. Program books thrusting a renewing church into society do not come out clean. Like the NCC's *Crisis in America* priority guide they seem handled into shape, decidedly the case with that document. Robert Theobald's initial drafts were, to say the least, sharp and bristling with awareness of crisis. The manuscript passed through so many hands and was honed to please so many minds that when the crisis priority was announced the book was not mentioned. It sold by the quantity. Perhaps somewhere there is a soul who was led to healing water. God knows, the priority program made so little impact that it received not a mention by Urban America and the Urban Coalition in a first anniversary progress report on implementation of Kerner Commission recommendations.

Departing from study books, there is a tendency to speak of church renewal in non-technical process language. Pope Paul's comments on the topic were listed under the rubric "task" in a collection of Vatican II speeches.[11] Dr. W. A. Visser 't Hooft, former general secretary of the World Coun-

cil of Churches, dealt with the "way" in the first of the
National Council-Paulist Press ecumenical *Living Room
Dialogues* in 1965.[12] "Journey"—inward and outward—was
Elizabeth O'Connor's description for the developments at
the innovating Church of the Saviour in Washington, D.C.[13]

The process-language tendency is extending by the more
recent trend merely to describe renewal experiments. William Holme's *Tomorrow's Church: A Cosmopolitan Community,* an outline of suburban renewal in Dallas, Texas,
represents expressed displeasure with renewal material offering nothing but "an assortment of intriguing hints and clues
for reshaping the church's structure as an institution."[14]

Rocking the Ark, a United Presbyterian case-book on nine
"traditional churches in the process of change"—a subtitle
which gets all the going terms—prefatorily asserts that "renewal is better described than defined; renewal is a process
and not a program; it can be pursued with equal validity in
a variety of ways."[15] While descriptions abandon abstraction,
most of the case studies put a disturbing stress on institutional
change. They lead more and more to the conclusion that the
church understands renewal as a means of saving itself. Mr.
Holmes' report is openly institutionally-oriented as are the
United Presbyterian descriptions.

Few case studies of Catholic renewal projects have been released in book form, though articles and news stories are
plentiful. Renewal consciousness entered Catholicism with
more deliberate, datable force than is true of Protestantism.
Within the Catholic Church, renewal is rather technically
the implementation of the recommendations coming from
popes and bishops in the Second Vatican Council. That it
has taken on broader identification is also true, as is almost
daily proven in the press. Catholic renewal, therefore, is

newer and more constrained and at its origin quite decidedly
an ecclesiastical matter geared to institution. The problems
which have arisen are "how far" as well as "what."

For Catholics, perhaps a part of the difficulty in determining where renewal is intended to go and how it operates
within a tight hierarchical structure comes from the ambiguity of *aggiornamento,* the word used by Pope John
XXIII when asked in 1959 why he was summoning an Ecumenical Council. (The Italian *aggiornamento* can quite literally mean "adjourn." Pope John certainly had the alternate
definition, "to bring up to date," in mind, although it is intriguing to speculate on the implications of the former. To
have called a Council so it might be adjourned would have
sufficiently frustrated both the advocates of conciliar church
government and its opponents.) A mandate to update nearly
two thousand years of accumulated dogma and structure is
no clear task, even with Council guidance.

Trouble in Catholic renewal is incontestable fact whether
its purpose is understood in continuity or discontinuity with
the past. Rebellion against the hierarchy is too commonplace
to need documentation. The conservative-minded could
make a case with Vatican II as culprit, breaching the walls
of both traditional piety and form and letting uninspected
cargo flowing in and out threaten the entire fortress. Since
the council officially *was,* such a view cannot in good will be
officially held. Father Gommar Depauw and his small, un-
recognized Catholic Traditionalist Movement refrain from
openly impugning the council.

Misunderstanding of Vatican II is more often cited as
reason for Catholicism's upheaval. Standing in mainstream
institutional renewal images, Cardinal Valerian Gracias of
Bombay capsuled considerable opinion by insisting in 1969
that the council initiated a process of renewal, but not a

reformation. "Pope John opened the window slightly," said the cardinal, "to let in fresh air, illustrating thus his *'aggiornamento'*; others are letting in a hurricane, so that the interested Catholic finds himself at times not only hanging on to his hat, but to his head as well!"

It may or may not be the "interested Catholic" doing the clutching, but clutch some are. Churchmen, like Cardinal Gracias, see no disjuncture between wanting renewal and lambasting those guilty of "pretense at recasting ancient religions and age-consecrated codes of morality."

Father Hans Küng, the Swiss theologian who has been in moderate crosscurrents to the Vatican, perceptively disagrees that the Council shoulders any blame for the Catholic Church's problems. He holds that modern turmoil would have happened without it. Father Küng looks at Vatican II as the Church's belated attempt to catch up with a spirit of democratization rooted in French and American constitutions and rejected by 19th century popes. Blaming Council or Pope John for recent developments, the priest-professor wrote in *The Critic,* is like blaming "a fire department for the fires which it attempts to quench."[16] "What is at fault . . . ," he said, "is the fact that the Council is not being taken seriously enough."

Whether Cardinal Gracias' conservative or Father Küng's liberal interpretation of the Council is accepted, Vatican II provides general Catholic self-consciousness about church renewal. Movement within, back from or beyond the council documents defines the choices The scene is different on the Protestant side of the aisle, where over 450 years of baptized diversity and pluralism offer a plethora of styles for the church's trek into the future. Attitudes toward renewal—negative and positive—are as multiple as the contents of Pandora's box.

Some of the attitudes, that is, underlying ideological and theological presuppositions, directing the care and feeding of renewal are treated in the following chapter. The data is no less than staggering. Before that, however, a word is needed about the distinction between *renewal* and *revolution*. Discussions of ecclesiastical change frequently employ the terms interchangeably, a practice which must be judged illegitimate. Neither linguistically nor operationally are they the same. Renewal is the process of up-dating and re-forming what is on hand. Revolution names a disruptive step in which something received and extant is pushed back. Its clearest synonym is "rebellion." Renewal's best synonym is "restore."

The rebelliousness of some contemporary Christian camps, particularly Catholic, is not renewal. Renewal, for example, existed before the "underground church" and the controversy over birth control. Renewal is the official position of pope, Vatican II and national conferences of bishops. "Underground church," Catholic guerilla-priests in Guatemala and non-juring theologians are more correctly reactions to renewal as institutional program. The Vatican will not return to 1870 mentality. Nor will it make Daniel Berrigan a bishop. Institutional Catholicism will stick to renewal as windows opened a crack to let in a limited amount of somewhat fresh air.

The community of Christian revolutionaries is in embryonic stages of growth. Even the National Federation of Priests' Councils, a U.S. group formed to exert influence on decision-making within Vatican II lines, considers itself a middle of the road voice. It aims at fostering reform and renewal instead of rebellion. There are probably more Catholic laymen than priests who are rebels. In percents, there are few rebellious Catholics of any kind.

A case could be made that whereas the Catholic leadership

wants to put the brakes on a change-happy laity, the opposite is the Protestant situation. While it is true that Protestant leaders have to push hard to stimulate laymen and most clergy to think or move, few of those leaders are revolutionaries. If they are less conservative than the mass of members, they are no less programmatic about renewal than the Catholic hierarchy. They do not aim to let church planning fall into the hands of conservatives whose lack of into-the-world thrust would eventually drown the church in the sea of cultural status quo. Renewalists in ecumenical Protestantism, on the other hand, only take tea with revolutionaries who would be pleased to see all denominational or interchurch structures dumped into a hole.

Historical Precedents

Renewal's basic character—Protestant or Catholic—can be disseminated from the two precedents most often cited, the pre-Constantinian church and the Reformation. The typological centrality of those two epochs are clear evidences of programmatic and restorative renewal consciousness. To be sure, the contemporary environment is taken into account, but it has seemed important that renewal not be *too* new. In short, a plastic age invites the pouring of new wine into old wineskins.

There can be much intellectual joy in finding renewal models in the early church where belief and practices of the faith demanded risk and commitment. Parallels can easily be drawn between pre- and post-Christendom. This can be done even if the danger of projecting another conquest of the social and political sphere—as with the Church of Imperial Rome—is avoided. A secular age which does not give too much attention to the church is comparable to the pagan age which ignored Christians except in spasmodic outbreaks of persecution. Likewise, a zealous church of the Apostles, Apostolic Fathers and apologists gives precedent to a modern church of intense commitment, service and beatific vision. Great, except that typology is not reality.

Seen as separate or intermixed, the church and the saeculum of the West have experienced each other for seventeen hundred years. The "world" cannot act as if it has not been infused with Christian presuppositions. As James Sellers said several years ago, osmosis has taken place on the rubbing edges of those inside and outside the church.[17] Further, the church cannot pretend it is new-born. The weight of tradition is too heavy. It is naive, even dumb, for a bishop in a mitre or a church bureaucrat in a nineteenth floor office suite to talk about returning to the simplicity of Jesus or St. John.

Given its inherited institutional forms, the church cannot play sect, not even if the structures are *re*formed and *re*vitalized. Rebellion, not renewal, would be absolutely mandatory before Christianity could be a sect hoping to leaven society's loaf. Sectarians do not, in initial stages of their movements, make pacts with reformers. They dissent, resist and generally have no time for experimenting with recipes of preservation.

The only way in which the modern church could recast itself in a first or second century mold would be by going sectarian. Revolutionaries in greater numbers than they now exist would be needed for this undertaking. The difficulty of a bring-up-to-date mentality within an inherited structure was keenly revealed in the experience of the now ended University Christian Movement. At least in name, the UCM in 1966 inherited what impetus was left in the National Student Christian Federation, "Y" programs, the National Newman Federation, an Orthodox Church student unit and sundry Protestant campus movements. There was a kind of sectarian

motivation in the organization, sectarian because of the concentration on a particular community, the university, and
sectarian because the movement was to be grass roots rather
than nationally legislated. Yet an attempt was made to maintain some top-echelon coordination functioning in relation
to denominational and ecumenical structures.

The thirty months of the UCM's life were hectic for the
national level organization which finally voted itself out of
existence. The action brought to a close over a century of
countrywide Christian student linkage and meant death for
one ecumenical experiment. Many reasons were undoubtedly
involved. Most often mentioned was the discovery that the
UCM simply could not carry out a program or fulfill its purposes. Reformulation of the university into a place of self-
identification—an undertaking with theological overtones—
was a major objective. Such a goal requires sectarian, if not
guerilla, tactics. One officer explained, upon the termination
of UCM, that as a national organization it could not partici-
pate in the life-death-resurrection struggle in any meaningful
way.

Born as an expression of ecumenizing renewal, UCM's decision to phase out was a rebellious gesture in opposition to
renewal's program-face. It was the recognition that grass roots
must be close to the soil, that models are built from the ground
up and not superimposed. Making the structure ecumenical,
loosening a few traditional bolts and adopting a new jargon
did not accomplish the job. Something newer was needed.
The UCM's apparent decision was that the novelty of no
national structure was worth a risk. A situation of no far-
flung organization does have overtones of pre-Christendom.

Utilizations of the Reformation as renewal precedent focus
mainly on Martin Luther, precursor of Protestantism. One
tale, perhaps apocalyptic, claims that when the Catholic bis-

hops arrived for the first session of Vatican II a banner flew somewhere in Rome bearing Luther's likeness and the caption, "In your heart you know he's right!" Luther's rightness in his own day is scarcely doubted today, even by Roman Catholics. Room remains to wonder if the fragmenting nature of developing Protestantism did not negatively overshadow the positive value of the reforming impetus. But that is a question for theological parlor games.

It is quite easy to see why Luther becomes hero in modern church renewal. He, and the Reformation as a whole, produced ecclesiastical change. To a degree Luther was involved in revolution, but only to a degree and in a particular context. His world-view was Christendom, and he strengthened instead of challenging the two-spheres theory of church and state cooperation. Luther was no more democratic in spirit than were Popes Leo X and Alexander VI. The Anabaptists—not Luther or Calvin or Zwingli—introduced rejection of church and state authority.

In terms of theological content and church form, of course, Luther was quite a rebel. When he is transported into contemporary Catholic-Lutheran dialogues or held up by the church for typological emulation he is most often Luther the renewalist, not wishing to destroy but to restore Pauline and Augustinian thought and revitalize structure.

However, as Jaroslav Pelikan has pointed ont, Luther proceeded from Spirit to structure, a course for reformation or renewal difficult for moderns more concerned with certainty about "the God of grace" than was Luther, whose stress was on "certainty about the grace of God."[18] Pelikan observes that the pattern might have to be shifted—proceeding from structure to Spirit—in 20th century reformation. Such is precisely the case, though renewalists very often attribute change to God while being totally unable to talk about God.

Still, Luther can be hero of contemporary renewal, for his
character, to use Pelikan's phrase, was formed in "the crisis
of Christian institutions."[19] Today's churchmen face institutional crises.

Though Pelikan sees Luther as always opposed to the
arbitrary imposition of structural authority on the freedom
of the Spirit and as equally against "free-floating subjectivity
of an individual. . ." there was some shift from the radical
early Reformer to the older man. In the course of Luther's
career, as Pelikan traces it, the resigned monk was confronted
with the structures he impugned in light of a need for structure. Pelikan finds a less radical, mature Luther, willing to
view as means of grace structures whose "divine institution
was not beyond question."

Much modern renewal begins not where Luther began
but launches forth from where he stopped. It is easier to re-
furbish and rearrange than to endure the full course of a
struggle between spirit and structure. Especially is this true
when there is no certainty of divine backing. And to many
renewal minds, redoing the shop seems quite as salvific as
would a coming of the Holy Spirit.

Notes

[1] Walter D. Wagoner, "Thoughts for Protestants to be Static By,"
The Christian Century (February 19, 1969), pp. 249-251. Wagoner gleans
his observations primarily from articles of Martin Marty.

[2] D. B. Robertson, *Should the Churches Be Taxed?* (Philadelphia:
The Westminster Press, 1968), p. 139.

[3] Nino Lo Bello, *The Vatican Empire* (New York: Trident Press,
1968), p. 135.

[4] Robertson, *op. cit.*, p. 168.

[5] *Ibid.*, citing Eugene Carson Blake, "Tax Exemption and the
Churches," *Christianity Today* (August 3, 1959), p. 7.

[6] Karl Rahner, *The Christian of the Future,* trans. W. J. O'Hara (New York: Herder & Herder, 1967), p. 77.

[7] *Ibid.,* pp. 78-79.

[8] Harvey Cox, *The Secular City* (New York: The Macmillan Company, 1965), paperback edition 1966, p. 127.

[9] *Crisis in America: Hope Through Action* (New York: Friendship Press, 1968).

[10] *Ibid.,* p. 5.

[11] *Council Speeches of Vatican II,* eds. Hans Küng, Yves Congar, O.P., and Daniel O'Hanlon, S.J. (Glen Rock, N.J.: Paulist Press, 1964).

[12] W. A. Visser 't Hooft, "The Way of Renewal," *Living Room Dialogues,* eds. William B. Greenspun, C.S.P., and William A. Norgren (Glen Rock, N.J.: Paulist Press and National Council of Churches, 1965), pp. 160-174. Reprinted from *The Renewal of the Church* (Philadelphia: The Westminster Press, 1957).

[13] Elizabeth O'Connor, *Journey Inward, Journey Outward* (New York: Harper & Row, 1968).

[14] William A. Holmes, *Tomorrow's Church: A Cosmopolitan Community* (Nashville: Abingdon Press, 1968), p. 7.

[15] Grace Ann Goodman, *Rocking the Ark* (New York: Division of Evangelism, Board of National Missions, United Presbyterian Church in the USA, 1968).

[16] Hans Küng, "Blame Everything on the Council," *The Critic* (February-March, 1969), p. 39.

[17] James E. Sellers, *The Outsider and the Word of God* (Nashville: Abingdon Press, 1961), pp. 14ff.

[18] Jaroslav Pelikan, *Spirit Versus Structure* (New York: Harper & Row, 1968), p. 137.

[19] *Ibid.,* p. ix.

2 / Attitudes toward Renewal

... and they lived, and stood upon their feet, an
exceedingly great host (Ezek. 37:10).

Immunity to renewal fever is an impossibility for all but the most geographically remote Christians. Somewhere in the heights of the Caucasus Mountains may be communities of Armenians untouched by modernity's waves. In only a certain few places in the European "first world," the North American "second world" or the all-the-rest "third world" have Catholics completely circumvented Vatican II fallout. The leaders of Orthodoxy, which in most lands is a Christian minority among Arabs or is under a Communist regime, are not unfamiliar with the theme of the 1968 Fourth Assembly of the World Council of Churches, "Behold . . . All Things New."

In the Reformation tradition Protestants of liberal persuasion are most supportive of renewing experimentation, but the conservatives and fundamentalists are not in splendid isolation. Reaction grants recognition. Moreover, the conservative-minded are pushing a renewal of their own, that is, the strengthening of metaphysical theism and the shoring up of zealous evangelical commitment to "biblical religion." This takes place partially in the wake of renewal's rudders.

W. A. Visser 't Hooft has provided a handy guide to attitudes toward or conceptions about renewal.[1] The task of explicating these threatens tedium. Some attempt, as breezy

25

as prudence permits, seems required for honesty's sake and in order to take into account the theological and cultural frames by which renewal is bounded. The treatment is scarcely exhaustive. It is representative, a glimpse of what churchmen would do with and about the fever in the bones. Visser 't Hooft did little more than mention six attitudes toward renewal. In the following sections, some of his examples are expanded and others are suggested.

Rejection of Church Renewal

The first attitude toward renewal cited by the Dutch ecumenist he illustrates with the position of Jacques Benigne Bossuet (1627-1704), the French Catholic bishop and historian. The claim that renewal of the *church* must be rejected and can be applied only to the piety and morality of individuals was issued as counteraction to Protestantism. Bossuet believed the Catholic Church remains perfected from its origin. He tried to apply this argument against the papacy in the conflict over privileges of the French Church. So assured was he of the invariability of the church that he staunchly defended the Gallican Declaration of 1682 which maintained a papal decision was not unalterable unless the church concurred.

Though Vatican II did not challenge the theory of papal supremacy and infallibility, it did raise the idea of conciliar authority to a high point and has led to increasing disregard for the pope's pronouncements. Bossuet's original thesis that renewal is limited to individuals was contradicted by the bishop's own Gallican period and by Vatican I and II. Consequently, Visser 't Hooft's Catholic example is somewhat irrelevant. Renewal as a personal matter is not presently a widespread Catholic concept. Individual and ecclesiastical expressions of religion are simply too interwoven. Besides, history refutes the notion that Catholicism thinks structures and practices are totally invariable. The attitude is more evident in contemporary Protestantism.

One of the fastest growing, yet least known, Protestant expressions is the collection of totally autonomous congregations known as the Churches of Christ. An early 20th century offshoot of the Disciples of Christ, the Churches of Christ make direct appeal to antiquity. Many church buildings bear a cornerstone declaring, "Founded 33 A.D." The New Testament provides authority. It would be unfair to say that none of the congregations of the primarily Southern movement have experienced renewal pangs. It is fair to say that should a renewal consciousness sweep the Churches of Christ —18,500 congregations with 2,356,800 members in 1965— emphasis would fall on individual piety and morality. Institutionally there is little to renew, a factor which partially explains why the existence of the Churches of Christ so seldom occur to Catholics or Protestants unless they happen to live as minorities in a county which has gone over, as detractors say, to the "Campbellites." (The term, incidentally, is derogatory only when applied to members of the Churches of Christ.)

Evangelist Billy Graham and confessingly evangelical Protestant denominations also treat renewal as personal, spiritual and moral uplift. Antiquity—"the Bible says"—again forms the foundation. Bossuet's assertion of the perfected nature of the church is, of course, missing in Graham presentations in which church is a matter to be dealt with after revival conversion. Evangelist Graham is careful not to give himself a denominational framework or image. He seldom talks about what the churches ought to do. By implication he, therefore, rejects direct institutional church renewal in favor of antiquity's models.

Renewal as Growth

The second attitude Visser 't Hooft posits is renewal in terms of development and growth, "of increasing realization of the inherent law of the living body."[2] There are both Roman Catholic and Protestant versions of this concept. The theory, or fact, of evolution lies behind it, a stance so deeply imbued in Western culture and religion that it often permeates positions receiving greater conscious stress. Visser 't Hooft himself illustrates traditional Protestant edginess with inherent law in his rejection of the idea that the church might of its own nature possess regenerative power apart from God's direction.

Protestants, however, can speak God's name first and then jump into progress-growth imagery about renewal minus divine sovereignty's propelling motion. Cultural conditioning is often responsible. Georgia Harkness, the United Methodist former seminary professor, is no believer in an inherent church renewal law. It can only be cultural saturation which caused her to quote the following lines from James Russell Lowell as relevant to church renewal's task:

> New occasions teach new duties;
> Time makes ancient good uncouth
> They must upward still, and onward,
> who would keep abreast of Truth.[3]

Lowell was basically an inherent law optimist. His concerns for "making man sole sponsor of himself" is context for the lines chosen by Miss Harkness. If applied to the church, the "sole sponsor" idea strikes an inherent law of development. Evolutionary renewal finds a happier and more honest

home among Catholics who can agree with J. A. Moehler
(1796-1838) on a process-theory for doctrinal development,
or find themselves followers of Teilhard de Chardin (1881-
1955) who drew little distinction between creation and provi-
dence. A recent proposal on renewal by Jesuit Fathers Edwin
M. McMahon and Peter R. Campbell takes an evolutionary
approach to church and theology which to some degree must
have been inspired by Teilhard de Chardin. In finding most
descriptions of renewal inadequate, McMahon and Campbell
state:

Perhaps in order to discover the true language of Christian experience we must penetrate deeper into the very dynamism of
human growth which underlies the constantly changing expressions of ourselves. Maybe it is something just this basic, something
shared by every human being simply because he is human, that
is needed as the starting point in Christian renewal.[4]

It is important to note that these men say "Christian renewal," not "church renewal." A developmental concept of
religious renewal is one which can make headway in Christianity apart from institutional forms. It is an infrequently
tried possibility.

Although not the case with McMahon and Campbell, hostility to the church can be a part of erstwhile Christian renewal
sated with itself. This is the case with certain of the radical,
secular theologies of the 1960's, those which partook in some
measure of classical optimism, the "best of all possible worlds"
poetry of Alexander Pope, and social Darwinism. Secular
theology, as Martin Marty has correctly observed, assumed
that man is a "problem-solving, controlling being."[5] Such was
William Hamilton's rendering of "death-of-God" theology.
In a 1965 essay in *The Christian Century*, he characterized

his appeal for Christians to assume worldly responsibility as radical and optimistic about human do-ability. He was much concerned about Christians discovering the meaning of life but little bothered about the revitalization of the church for which he initially said he felt indifference.

Hamilton's later decision to entertain the possibility of a relation between radical theology and the church probably had no cause-effect impact on others who decided to do precisely that. A can-do, can-control, can-solve consciousness of man's inherent social and personal nature pervades much renewal talk which begins with detailed mission strategy, part of which is concern about other persons and part of which is an institutionally unradicalized edition of Hamiltonian optimism. Insofar as renewal has, for a fact, been accompanied by greater church thrusts into political and social arenas, the multiplicity of church and ecumenical proclamations to the social order represent a kind of realization of an inherent law of the body. It seems right to *become* a verbal protestor and demand-maker because it seems right that the church should develop outward.

Renewal as Conformity

The third renewal concept Visser 't Hooft cites is one he calls the "modernist movements . . . (whose) claim is that the renewal of the Church must take the form of an adaptation to the new cultural developments and that not merely at the level of formulation and structural patterns, but at the level of the content of the faith." The former World Council executive dislikes this and issues a Pauline caution peppering "conformity to the world."[6]

Secular theologies come immediately to mind under this rubric. It would, however, be incorrect to brand as conformity all theology or ecclesiastical proposals utilizing "secular" simply because the term means "of the age." Visser 't Hooft escapes the dilemma of showing examples of conformist renewal by half-mentioning a liberal German Protestant movement of the 1860's. The best illustrations of accommodation to the world minus Christian content are found in periods of church lethargy, liberal or conservative, which allow cultural situations to dominate. Most of German Protestantism and Catholicism in the early Hitler period, some churches in modern South Africa and American denominations spouting racism come to mind; or there is the confusing of Christianity with Americanism, the kind of civic religion clouding the U.S. at and after the inauguration of President Richard Nixon.

Since "renew" is the linguistic opposite of "lethargy," conformist church renewal is faddism rather than an obedience to mainstream culture. Faddistic church renewal is manifold though, again, theology employing secular images is not an automatic definition. A secularist passion in church or theology can be healthy. It guards against other-worldly religiosity. Both God-centeredness and humanism suffer when separated from each other. The entire issue of secularization in modern Christianity would not have caused such shocking consternation had Dietrich Bonhoeffer's much-hailed "religionless" and "man's coming of age" been kept in the Christocentric framework in which he did all his writing.[7] A man in prison for plotting in love to assassinate a heinous tyrant, Hitler, must be allowed the privilege of probing the way of his soul without lesser witnesses, who have never suffered, making him a paragon.

Bonhoeffer's "man's coming of age" did not have in his circumstances the same ring of jubilation which Englishmen and Americans came to hear in it. Still, Bishop J. A. T.

Robinson's strange Bonhoeffer-Tillich-Bultmann admixture asking for some Christian honesty had value.[8] The same is true of the first half of Harvey Cox's *The Secular City*, wherein the modern saeculum is described.[9]

After the word "secular" came into vogue, theology did the same thing theology always does with a co-opted expression. It was journalized and transposed from description to content. Or worse, it was turned into a gimmick. The church has a weakness for gimmicks, as any here's-how book on evangelism or supply-house catalogue demonstrates. Not secularization itself—an established fact—but what the jargonists did with it represents a brand of renewal which sells conformity. The conformity is not to the world but to the jargon.

"Church in the world" is for some a veritable confession of faith, the content of belief, rather than a directional statement. This is particularly true in the Protestant-Catholic ecumenical movement. Unable to proceed very far with doctrinal or structural dialogues, everyone of "good will" can, at best, put shoulders to the wheel of world economic development and relief and, at worse, can put tongue to phrase. These undertakings are noble. Nevertheless, it must be doubted that the church has much of a unique place in the world as an agency of economic prowess. If church and ecumenical movement cannot deal with the question of God, neither has any reason to exist, and if ecumenism can only talk, it is better never commenced.

The gimmicky use of "secular" has been depicted in a rash of books and articles which use it in titles. Some are merely transparent efforts to cash in on the commercial value of a going thing. Others are well-intentioned modism. A trick is being played on a reader when a supposedly secular theologian or writer comes up with the doctrines and structures for faith in a religionless world which can be found, stripped of hip words, in the outline of Calvin's *Institutes*. The steps after "secular church," "secular saint," "secular Christ" and "secular faith" are "secular curia," "secular synod" and "secular Bible." Grand word games are not church renewal.

Currently, the entire secular syndrome is undergoing severe criticism by some of the better minds, although *Newsweek* magazine's intimation last February that labor to "fashion a secular religion" had been abandoned was more projective than real.[10] Unfortunately, the church runs considerably behind *Newsweek*, and the end of secular pumping is not yet. Martin Marty in his *The Search for a Usable Future*,[11] and Peter Berger in *A Rumor of Angels*,[12] in different ways, point away from the secularist preoccupations. Marty elucidates the sociological flaws in secular theology. One of his conclusions is that secularists miscalculate optimism's capacity to parallel human experience. Berger, a sociologist, sketches a viable approach to a religious understanding of the dimensions of transcendence as man's common life points beyond itself. Sociology, of course, could be merely the next item on theology's co-opt list.

As a discipline dealing with life the way it is experienced, sociology offers significant data to church renewalists. A major renewal incentive has been to alter the psychological drift away from Christianity, which the sociologists document. Sensitivity would also seem to dictate that churchmen let sociology tell them how the process is going. The reports are not glowing with health. To Berger, many theological minds are "awed" by the modern world and too ready to jump on intellectual bandwagons. Why is this not good? Because, Berger says, it does not serve to illuminate the "signals of transcendence" which are humanly experienced and, consequently, can be the starting point for a genuinely relevant theology.[13] His concern is not to preserve anything extant, such as church, just because it is there. Berger's appeal is for church and theology to begin with the basic question of how human experience may be understood in relation to that transcending it. The suggestion is valid in a culture in which the sociologists can show that churches—yea, renewing ones—are empty of meaning for most persons.

Renewal as Futuristic or Utopian

Visser 't Hooft's fourth and fifth views of renewal spring, respectively, from Protestant orthodoxy and from sectarianism—any brand. The fourth believes that church renewal cannot be realized until the "new dispensation," that is, the Second Coming of Christ is realized. The fifth is actualization upon earth of perfected church in the manner of the ancient Montanists, the 16th century Anabaptists, classical Mormonism, some Adventists, and revelationists of all types. Historically, this latter expression is on the fringe of Christianity and will receive no further mention as such. Sectarian renewal in the modern age does, however, exist, although its nature is less utopian than older examples. New style sectarian church renewal is cliquish, sometimes arrogant about its relevance. It will be discussed specifically in the second section of this book.

Neither are eschatological renewalists of the orthodox type literally a part of the church renewal movement under consideration here. Those waiting for God's in-breaking into history include numerous Protestants but not nearly so many as a generation ago. The view depends on a literalistic interpretation of the New Testament. A Jeffrey Hadden survey of several thousand Protestant clergymen—Methodist, Episcopal, Presbyterian, American Baptist, American Lutheran and

Missouri Synod Lutheran—showed that less that 50 per cent, except for the Missouri Synod, believed in a near literal interpretation of the Scripture.[14] Moreover, an increasingly social consciousness and general worldly stirring in congregations of the Southern Baptist Convention indicate that this large segment of conservative U.S. Protestantism is not so otherworldly as formerly.

The futuristic reference introduces an opportunity to consider in relation to church renewal the newer non-apocalyptic eschatology known as "the theology of hope." This is no place for a critique of the thought of Jurgen Moltmann, the German who is its foremost exponent. It must suffice to say that in moving eschatology from the bottom to the top of theology's table of contents he unleashed creative possibilities for Christians journeying into the future which neither the old orthodoxy nor secular theology has done. Moltmann was, of course, wrongly seen as answer-man to the "death-of-God" theology in 1968 American press presentations. His "theology of hope" developed in Europe at the same time the radical secularists were holding forth in the U.S. Insofar as both Moltmann and the secularists reacted to traditional piety gone stale, the "theology of hope" is an alternate to the "death-of-God."

Moltmann is impatient in *The Theology of Hope* with "religion as the cult of the subjective," "religion as the cult of co-humanity" and "religion as the cult of the institution."[15] He does not discuss church renewal per se, but ends his book by asserting that disclosure of "the horizon of the future of the crucified Christ" to a world of lost horizons is the church's task.[16]

A theology agreeing with Ernst Bloch in understanding God as having "future as his essential nature," can only, as Moltmann does, deal with community or church in exodus images. "Christianity has its essence and its goal not in itself and not in its own existence, but lives from something and exists for something which reaches far beyond itself."[17] The eschatological community of believers can see the present world as free from "all attempts at self-redemption or self-production through labour, and it becomes open for loving, ministering self-expenditure in the interests of a humanizing of conditions and in the interests of the realization of justice in the light of the coming justice of God."[18] It would follow that the church would be freed from efforts to preserve or protect itself.

The force which Moltmann's "theology of hope" may have on what is already established as a church renewal movement remains a future question. Rhetoric of hope has entered the stream. A new dish of "process theology" by Kenneth Cauthen tacks "theology of hope" onto the end of metaphysical organism and offers it to "church and culture as a viable option for man seeking meaning and fulfillment."[19] More substantial are Martin Marty's ponderings over a future having "theology *with* hope." He is not sure any "theology of hope" can bear the weight of the needs of the future. No programmatic renewalist, Marty avoids a discussion of how institutional church might operate in a future with hope except to say that it will have a risk-script.[20]

Those in the modern world doing the most risking are those with most reasons to hope for changed social—not religious—situations: African nationalists, Latin American revolutionaries, students and American blacks. In the Black Church in the U.S. there is example of renewal *with* a theology of hope. Explication can be centered on Albert Cleage and his Shrine of the Black Madonna (United Church of Christ) in Detroit. Cleage's word, "revolution," cannot be totally divorced from renewal, for he is a churchman and

more literally a semi-revolutionary. While real Malcolm X
followers and some Black Panthers reject the religion of
former masters. Cleage stoutly claims Christianity, albeit a
black interpretation. He views the Black Church in American
history as continuously relevant to the needs of black people.
In the revolutionary period in which the late 20th century
black community finds itself, he wants the church to be revolutionary, that is, renewed from serving black needs symbol-
ized by problem-escaping in "down-home" Sunday services
where hope was in a celestial city. He wants the church to
serve the needs of the black man now in social and political
revolution.

To accomplish this, Cleage has set forth a black theology.
The foremost ingredient is the "black Messiah."[21] This represents not only a black historical Jesus but also a mission to
the black people. The idea of a black messianic mission to the
whites is not far behind what Cleage says, and not so far-
fetched.

Exodus figures of speech abound in Cleage's sermons, as
they did in the speeches of the late Martin Luther King, Jr.
Cleage disagreed with King on approaches to the problems of
blacks, yet both predated Moltmann in utilizing futuristic,
promise-filled and hopeful language about church and Christian life. Is it fair to label King a church renewalist? Probably
not, at least not in the same way that some lay forth programs
for local church restructure. King, however, is never correctly
understood apart from his role as preacher. Throughout the
course of his adult career, he was pastor as well as civil rights
leader and Nobel Peace Prize laureate. The church was pre-
supposed frame of reference. He was minister to black congregations in an integrated denomination, the American Baptist
Convention. King was never outside what he criticized
when he blasted churches for preaching segregation or praised

them for strides toward integration. He saw the institutional church with an eye for renewal when he said in 1967: "Today the judgment of God is upon the church for its failure to be true to its mission. If the church does not recapture its prophetic zeal, it will become an irrelevant social club without moral or spiritual authority."[22] The challenge could apply to black, all-white or integrated denominations. It was a renewal—spiritually and institutionally—with hope which King envisioned.

Renewal as God-following

The final concept of renewal mentioned by Visser 't Hooft, the one he chooses to follow, is man responding to God's initiative for the repentance, liberation and reedification of the church. This attitude characterizes mainstream Protestant ecumenism and is the one most pushed by Protestant denominations. It has permeated the motto-making level of the World Council of Churches from Amsterdam in 1948 to Uppsala in 1968. Two years before the Amsterdam organizational meeting, the Council's provisional committee chose "Man's Disorder and God's Design" as the theme. Since Visser 't Hooft was a key figure in setting up the World Council, it is not difficult to know why he elects the God-following man-repenting way of renewal. Human disorder is to be turned from; God's plan is to be emulated.

Ecumenical church renewal, to which the World Council testifies and into which Catholicism is being drawn, considered four topics under the general theme of the Amsterdam Assembly: The Universal Church in God's Design, The Church's Witness to God's Design, The Church and the Disorder of Society and The Church and the International Disorder. A preface to the advance documents of Amsterdam explained the significance of these topics:

They represent burning concerns of all the churches in this crisis of civilization. The first reveals the growing determination of the various churches to rediscover the divine intention for the Church, and the right relationship of the various churches to one another. . . . The second testifies to the obligation recognized by all churches alike to claim for Christ the whole world and all aspects of life. From the outset it has been recognized that the World Council would be still-born unless evangelism were its life-blood. The third and fourth subjects bring Christian faith directly to bear upon two critical areas of disorder in contemporary civilization, the social and the international. They deal with the familiar query: What has the Church to contribute to society in its present extremity?[23]

The World Council has undergone substantial change since 1948, but the Amsterdam consciousness has served as underlying program. A pledge was made at Amsterdam to "stay together" in seeking God's intention, claiming the whole world and finding out what church can contribute to society. The vow was expanded at the Evanston Assembly in 1954 to include a dedication to God "that He may enable us to grow together." According to the World Council publication in 1967, the New Delhi Assembly of 1961 left the delegates with a "sense of the progress that had been made." Uppsala in 1968 proclaimed with Revelation 21:5, "Behold, . . . all things new. . .", the subject apparently being God rather than the World Council.

Languagewise, an easy-stepping trepidation at Amsterdam was replaced by confidence of vision at Uppsala. The implication is that the World Council had learned how to repent of man's disorder, to be liberated and follow God's initiative. Or, pragmatically, it may mean that institutional maturity may simply lead to bolder statement.

World Council type renewal has strongly influenced denominational approaches. A 1967 United Church of Christ local group study guide called *The Church Swept Out* concluded with a chapter using the Uppsala theme, "All Things New."[24] Author Ralph Weltge's "road of renewal" is like Visser 't Hooft's—God, repentance, newness (liberation), and mission in unity (reedification). The report from a three-year United Presbyterian investigation of "Renewal and Extension of the Church's Ministry in the World" begins without Amsterdam phraseology. Not far down, however, is the stipulation that everything except commitment to Christ (the God awareness) must be risked for renewal; obedience (repentance) is called essential and life must be lost to find it (reedification). Then a sentence reads: "renewal is going on by God's radical action, even though churchmen may resist." It is "man's disorder and God's design" all over again on local and denominational levels.

Going forth under the configuration of God to abolish human chaos is noble theory. Noble practice, too, if the goal is accomplished. On higher ecumenical and denominational levels, church renewal has assumed a pro-liberal attitude toward social improvement. A specific topic is civil rights in the U.S. Integration of Negroes and whites came to be generally identified with God's design in the early 1960's. Segregation represented man's disorder.

The time is past due for renewalists to ask how much overcoming of racism has been accomplished. Obviously, the answer is very little. A NORC Amalgam Survey of Protestant laymen in 1967 showed that 43 per cent under thirty-five years of age and 48 per cent over fifty-five disapproved of the

Negro civil rights movement. A Jeffrey Hadden poll of Protestant clergy in the same year showed a maximum of 8 per
cent disapproving.[25] The implication is that church professionals are easier to renew than other people.

Should "God's design" renewal be conceived as liberaliza-
tion of those who run churches, it probably succeeds very
well. A mission to clergy, however, is only one small aspect
of this approach intended to infiltrate the entirety of the
churches' constituencies. Perhaps more time is the answer.
But the church does not have more time to show the merit
of racial integration. Already the mood of resegregation has
set in, partly because the white man's chaos was not brought
under a just design. Some who pushed integration a decade
ago have begun to preach separation for the Negroes' own
good. And both under God's design. For laymen it must be
confusing to hear one top churchman singing "We Shall
Overcome" while another of equal importance sings "Black
is Beautiful." The desegregation-resegregation conversation
gives pause to wonder if God's design is multiple. Or if it is
known at all?

A Word on the Orthodox

Though many Protestant executives seem often to forget,
the renewing wind of World Council and National Council
ecumenism officially encompasses the Churches of Eastern
Orthodoxy. The Ecumenical Patriarchate of Constantinople
—spiritual locus in the *primus inter pares* relationship of
the Orthodox Church—expressed ecumenical fervor in the
1920's and was an originating part of the World Council of
Churches. Most of the other ancient patriarchal seats and the
several autonomous or autocephalous churches came into
the ecumenical picture at the New Delhi World Council

Assembly. By the time of Uppsala, Orthodox delegates comprised the largest confessional family in the Council.

Western attention to Orthodoxy and Orthodoxy's own awareness of the West received greatest incentive in the three mid-1960's visits between Pope Paul and Ecumenical Patriarch Athenagoras I. Preliminary to the unprecedented occasions were the mutual liftings of excommunications of popes and patriarchs which had existed since 1054.

Friendly contact between leaders and World Council membership is not the same as internal church renewal. The chance for an active Orthodox renewal movement has been hampered by the political realities in which Orthodox Churches find themselves. Except for the jurisdictions in the Americas, no Orthodox Church is free of political restraints. (The Church of Greece is technically free but remains under tight state control.) The four ancient patriarchates, Constantinople (Istanbul), Antioch, Jerusalem and Alexandria, are in countries controlled by non-Christians. With the exception of the relatively few recent months when Jerusalem has been governed by Israel, the patriarchates have for centuries been in Islamic lands where religious freedom is not an inalienable right. The Ecumenical Patriarch's presence in Istanbul has been an embarrassment to Turkey and is seldom without pressure. The Patriarchate is protected by the 1927 Treaty of Lausanne. There have been recent hints of more cordial relations between Orthodoxy's spiritual capital and the heirs of the caliphs. However, in 1967 the Turkish press barely mentioned the fact that Pope Paul came to see Patriarch Athenagoras. The papal presence was duly noted as though he was visiting the Turks.

The predominantly historic Orthodox nations of Europe—minus Greece—are all under Communist domination. These Churches are surprisingly healthy today, even in Russia, but are limited in terms of worldwide contacts and self-direction. The leaders of the Russian Orthodox Church sometimes seem to have considerable freedom, enough so that Metropolitan Nikodim of Leningrad and Novodsky, chairman of the Church's department of foreign affairs, could say at the WCC's Uppsala Assembly that Christianity can never surrender to Communism. At the same time, the Russian Church cannot send funds to Geneva to support the World Council. One example of how it tries to make financial contributions came in 1968 when a key pre-Uppsala panel went to Zagorsk to hold a meeting. The Russian Church paid almost the entire cost of the gathering, including transportation.

Failure of the churches to die under several decades of Communist control is received in some quarters as a symbol of hope for the church at large. There is worth in this observation—the insight that the church does not have to be in a favored social position to exist. It is a better situation for the church to carry on because some men want it—as in Eastern Europe—than to be carried on because men have it.

It is only within the Church of Greece and the American Orthodox jurisdictions that anything closely resembling Protestant and Catholic renewal can take place. Greece since World War II has been plagued with political upheaval. Rampant traditionalism reigned in the Church until mid-1967 when, after the military coup, the now ruling Archbishop Ieronymos was named Primate of Athens and All Greece. Under the deposed Archbishop Chrysostomos relations with the Ecumenical Patriarchate and with the ecumenical movement had been strained. The new archbishop smoothed contacts with Patriarch Athenagoras, and it was hoped that the good spirit of ecumenism evident in his enthronement address would come to characterize the Greek Church's foreign policy. This hope was at least temporarily shattered when the Commission of the Churches on International Affairs, a World Council agency, announced plans to seek an expert to review the then proposed new Greek Constitution. Especially at issue was concern over treatment of political prisoners, alleged to be held by the score by the military government putting forward the constitution. This, coupled with remarks by Swedish Premier Tag Erlander supporting the cause of ousted Greek Premier George Papandreou, resulted in a Greek Church boycott of the World Council Assembly in Uppsala. This was one instance when the Council's claim to "the whole world and all aspects of life" would have been better served in silence.

Archbishop Ieronymos and a revamped Holy Synod have set about to modernize some aspects of Orthodoxy in Greece. The new constitution, reviewed by the Synod before presentation to the people, provided for a new Church Charter allowing greater self-determination than ever before. An attempt to fill hundreds of vacant priestly posts was commenced, and the possibility of abolishing required beards and cassocks for priests has been verbally entertained. Periodic purges of the clergy and hierarchy and the apparently forced resignations of some bishops, considered the most progressive, remain unexplained. Announced intentions of religious revitalization are frequent. Pluralism is still frowned upon. The conclusion must be that Orthodoxy in Greece is now undergoing the birth pangs of some kind of renewal whose future course is unclear.

Orthodoxy is recognized as the fourth major religious expression in the U.S. where, to large degree, it maintains ethnic identities. Greek Orthodoxy, directly related to the Ecumenical Patriarchate, and Russian Orthodoxy, of several sorts, are the largest groups numerically. Ecumenical contacts with Catholics and Protestants have steadily grown. Attempts to combine the American jurisdictions, a proposal favorably suggested by the Standing Conference of Canonical Orthodox Bishops in the Americas, has not been well received by a commission planning an early 1970's third Pan-Orthodox World Conference. Two such previous meetings on the Island of Rhodes made significant headway in bringing spiritual unity and greater cooperation among the Orthodox Churches.

Church structures in American Orthodoxy are tightly hierarchical. Defections from the clergy, in contrast to Protestantism and Catholicism, are rare. Yet in some geographic areas of heavy Orthodox populations, the degree of church participation is very low. There are few situations which might be termed "experimental ministries." One Mid-West based renewal group in the Greek Orthodox Archdiocese received a setback when the priest-editor of a publication was temporarily suspended. The action by an ecclesiastical court was said to have been taken not because the editor disagreed with or criticized the archdiocese and its leader, Archbishop Iakovos, but because the disagreement was expressed in public, journalistic form rather than through church channels.

Archbishop Iakovos marched alongside Martin Luther King, Jr. on the Selma bridge-crossing in 1965 and has consistently championed the cause of racial justice. He has also tried to instill an American consciousness into his people to stand beside appreciation of their Hellenic background. American Orthodoxy has not, however, pushed out into social and political territories as Protestantism and Catholicism have. Somewhat parochial, political conservatism is strong, as evidenced by the tumultuous ovation given a telegram from then

Vice-Presidential candidate Spiro T. Agnew when the greeting was read at the third annual Name Day celebration for Archbishop Iakovos in early November, 1968.

Renewal in Orthodoxy is decidedly a spiritual emphasis, and it shall be many years before any Orthodox Church issues a booklet on process and change called "Rocking the Ark."

Notes

[1] W. A. Visser 't Hooft, "The Way of Renewal," from *The Renewal of the Church* (Philadelphia: The Westminster Press, 1957). Reprinted in *Living Room Dialogues*, eds. William B. Greenspun, C.S.P., and William A. Norgren (Glen Rock, N.J.: Paulist Press and the National Council of Churches, 1965), pp. 160-174. Cited from the latter.

[2] *Ibid.*, p. 161.

[3] Georgia Harkness, *Stability Amid Change* (Nashville: Abingdon Press, 1969), p. 28, citing James Russell Lowell's "The Present Crisis," stanza 18.

[4] Edwin M. McMahon and Peter A. Campbell, *The In-Between: Evolution in Christian Faith* (New York: Sheed & Ward, 1969), p. 8.

[5] Martin E. Marty, *The Search for a Usable Future* (New York: Harper & Row, 1969), p. 31.

[6] Visser 't Hooft, *op. cit.*, p. 162.

[7] Bonhoeffer spoke both of "man" and the "world" "come" and "coming" of age. The scholarly wing which makes its living wondering what he meant, whether he was reporting or prophesying, provides interesting reading, but obviously is of the temperament which takes phrases out of context. In outlining a book he wished to write, Bonhoeffer used "religionless" and "man . . . come of age" in a context where both clearly mean self-sufficient mankind free from nature. *Cf.*, *Letters and Papers from Prison*, revised edition, ed. Eberhard Bethge (New York: The Macmillan Company, 1967), pp. 208ff. He described, at least, human intention. He was not, however, happy about an advanced stage of maturity unless there is consciousness of "existence for others," for which Jesus Christ is prototype.

[8] John A. T. Robinson, *Honest To God* (Philadelphia: The Westminster Press, 1963).

9 Harvey Cox, *The Secular City* (New York: The Macmillan Company, 1965).

10 Kenneth L. Woodward, "The Supernatural Reality," *Newsweek* (February 24, 1969), p. 56.

11 Martin E. Marty, *op. cit.*

12 Peter L. Berger, *A Rumor of Angels* (Garden City: Doubleday & Company, 1969).

13 *Ibid.,* p. 65ff.

14 Jeffrey K. Hadden, *The Gathering Storm in the Churches* (Garden City: Doubleday & Company, 1959), p. 39.

15 Jurgen Moltmann, *Theology of Hope,* trans. James W. Leitch (New York: Harper & Row, 1967), pp. 311ff.

16 *Ibid.,* p. 338.

17 *Ibid.,* p. 325.

18 *Ibid.,* p. 338.

19 Kenneth Cauthen, *Science, Secularization and God* (Nashville: Abingdon Press, 1969), p. 9. *Cf.,* pp. 222-229.

20 Marty, *op. cit.,* pp. 141ff.

21 Albert Cleage, *Black Messiah* (New York: Sheed & Ward, 1968).

22 Martin Luther King, Jr., *Where Do We Go from Here: Chaos or Community?* (New York: Harper & Row, 1967), p. 96.

23 *Man's Disorder and God's Design: The Amsterdam Assembly Series* (New York: Harper & Brothers, 1948), general preface.

24 Ralph Weltge, *The Church Swept Out* (Philadelphia: United Church Press, 1967), pp. 82ff.

25 Hadden, *op. cit.,* pp. 104, 148.

3 / The Road from Yesterday

Behold, they say, Our bones are dried up, and
our hope is lost; we are clean cut off (Ezek. 37:11).

The spectrum of church renewal activity and theory did not spring full-grown out of churchmen's heads. It has lineage: theological, ecclesiastical and nonreligious. The inevitable movement of time bears major responsibility. Any attempt to give a specific date to its inception is bound to fail. Generally, and in its present multiplicity, church renewal in the United States is a post-World War II product only vaguely predictable when sons and husbands returned home from Europe and the South Pacific in the late 1940's. Religiously, World War II to a degree did for the U.S. what World War I did for Europe: it bent the back of theological optimism— pre-"secular city" variety—about man's goodness. Contrary to many assessments, human optimism never goes completely out of vogue. So strong has it been in the U.S. that the dip precipitated by the war took some years to surface.

World War II devastated America's tendency toward isolationism which had continued after the first "great" 20th century war. It etched memories of horror in men's minds. It caused a fast-paced economy. Doubts about the effectiveness and relevance of traditionally accepted ideas began to creep into society with greater rapidity. Theologians found cause to have second thoughts about a host of matters. Twentieth century man commenced a reassessment of himself.

48

A change in human self-conception is usually indicative of a forthcoming period of religious transition. Ancient Israel experienced this transition as it changed from a nomadic self-awareness and became a settled people in Palestine. Christians' conscious identification as "citizens" instead of "criminals" following the legalizing edict of Constantine in the 4th century prepared the way for the nonpersecuted Imperial Church which kept a watchful eye on every sphere of life. The expansion of human knowledge in the Renaissance was complicatedly and closely tied to the Protestant Reformation. Physical and astronomical discoveries which altered views of man's place in the universe prior to and during the 18th century Enlightenment produced deistic Protestants and "Modernist" Catholics.

Nineteenth century Darwinism disquieted some and angered others but also led to evolutionary conceptions of religion, progressivistic historical theories and optimistic visions of man's future. That is where a large segment of Christendom sat when the lid blew off in 1914. The rest of the church was staid in orthodoxies: Catholic, Lutheran, Reformed or sectarian. Vanguarders—the optimists—and not rearguarders got the bayonets in World War I. The liberals, not the conservatives, were the first to be figuratively shot down. But that was all in Europe. Religion in America was scarcely affected by World War I.

Europe was in turmoil between the wars. So was Protestantism, especially in Germany to which Protestant eyes had long looked for theological and ecclesiastical inspiration. Catholicism remained unmoved, secure behind the walls of the 16th century Council of Trent and the dogmatic decrees of the First Vatican Council of 1870. Popes had recently experienced political setbacks in Italy, but Rome was spiritually unchallenged from within.

High echelons of German-speaking Protestants were undergoing the first waves of what would later be variously called Neo-orthodoxy, Neo-Protestantism or dialectical theology, the prime mover of which was Karl Barth. The Swiss theologian rejected most tenets of liberal Protestantism as irrelevant to a world so recently washed in blood. Far from being a political or social treatise, Barth's 1919 *Epistle to the Romans* was heavily theological. Basically, he declared that church or theology which relies on innate human ability to know or to do God's will is wrong. Protestant liberalism had tended toward such optimism. Barth put the stress on God's sovereignty and elevated the church, in certain dimensions, above time, place or historical circumstances.

Barth's innovation is now hailed as *cataclysmic hiatus*, but in 1919 most of the thunder was in the German universities. No Christian reawakening was to emerge from Switzerland to sweep over Europe, and most Americans could not read German and knew little about Barth until Douglas Horton and others introduced his thought much later.

On the whole the church in Europe was dormant between 1914 and the Hitler era in terms of its impact on people. The uneasiness Barth felt with old orthodoxy and liberalism —and which he could theologically articulate—was also known among part of the populace, with whom it often went deeper than choice between established religious ideology and new theological proposal. Many abandoned the church altogether. Marxism flourished. Nihilism increased. After all, Europe had well-laid non-church fires fanned by Voltaire, Nietzsche and the early Marxists. And stagnated churches making no attempt to guide men in trying times were matters of fact. Catholicsm was rote. Martin Luther's efforts to enliven religious understanding with vernacular Scripture, widespread Christian education and common-language liturgy had long been dogmatized. John Wesley's burning zeal, bequeathed to the English Methodists, had dimmed. Friedrich Schleiermacher's inward-looking theology was a forerunner of the liberalism against which Barth and others were reacting.

The coming of Hitler and National Socialism to Germany in the 1930's precipitated signs of new life in the anti-Nazi German Confessing Church. Barth was instrumental in this revival. Traditional Lutheran and Reformed Orthodoxy, tacitly held by the masses, were swept aside in the political storm. Optimism was unthinkable. The Confessing Church became involved with the political and social struggle despite the hardships and death inflicted upon many leaders of the movement. Pastor Martin Niemoller became a hero in U.S. denominational mission study books.

There was not in German Catholicism as marked an anti-Nazi wing as was the Confessing Church in Protestantism. A partial reason was the non-opposition Concordat with the Third Reich signed by the Vatican. Yet the valiant opposition to Hitler of Catholic Action, a lay movement, should not be overlooked.[1]

Europe was doubly tired and in shambles after the second war. Communism was no longer an abstract philosophy or an experiment in Russia. In 1918 Eastern Orthodoxy in Russia had been virtually wiped out by the Communist takeover. The same threat hung over the Protestant, Catholic and Orthodox Churches of the rest of Eastern Europe as the Soviet Union steadily gained sway over the region after 1945.

Protestant Renewal

Protestantism had the World Council of Churches to foster and form in 1948. The significance of the World Council in the course of renewal interests must not be minimized. It represents a kind of Christian cooperation which has made possible Christian venturing into social-political spheres and into new ecclesiastical forms. Despite the Council's constant claims that it does not push organic union of churches, the spirit of cooperation it symbolizes has made merger of structures or programs attainable.

The World Council originated out of missionary zeal, evangelism, rather than from any deliberate attempt to renew the existing church. Its history began with the World Missionary Conference of 1910 in Edinburgh. Spawned by Edinburgh were two movements, Faith and Order and Life and Work (now Church and Society), which pushed Christian cooperation beyond traditional missions. These two came together in 1948 to establish the Council. Emerging so near the end of World War II, the first WCC Assembly in Amsterdam had the nature of a "what next" round table.

Anticipation of renewal on the European front was voiced by Jacques Ellul in an Amsterdam preliminary paper. He indicted the Churches, Protestant and Catholic, for unintentionally leaving to others the protection of humans, responsibility for revolution and the spiritual nurture of peoples and nations. Ellul concluded that evidence showed the "church had no clear view of its divine mission, and was not constantly on the alert to hear God's message." He called for rediscovery of a three-fold responsibility of the church to protect bodies and minds, to maintain a mission of "permanent revolution" and to be sensitive to spirits foreshadowed by the rhetoric, if not the activity, of the future.[2]

The Amsterdam report on the U.S. corresponding to Ellul's on Europe was given by Reinhold Niebuhr. It did not mention the church but concentrated on the continuation in American life of strong reliance on classical political-economic liberalism and laissez faire philosophy. He noted that reality could diverge from the ideal without killing hope, that a return to prior conditions would be possible after the "aberrations of war-time disciplines was anticipated by many Americans."[3]

It did seem after World War II that the church could also go back to the security of one pluralistic nation under God, run mainly by white Protestants. The U.S. had suffered without trembling in the war. Where was the overwhelming evidence of church failure? Niebuhr said that American society as a whole "might be tempted to cling too desperately to the belief in an automatic harmony of social forces and thereby fail to take such steps in time as are required to manage the vast and dynamic forces of a technical society in the interest of justice and stability."[4]

That warning has probably come true, but it was only the pessimism of a controversial theologian in post-war America. Religion boomed following the war. Nearly 300,000 lives had been lost, but victory was at hand and the still young nation was the unchallenged leader of a "free world." Along with triumph on the battlefield came burgeoning church membership and attendance. The times were compared to the frontier revivals of the 18th and 19th centuries. Seminaries were filled. Billy Graham emerged as a sex symbol as well as dispenser of certain salvation. Norman Vincent Peale was positively the rage and Bishop Fulton J. Sheen was successfully competing with Jack Benny for television ratings. Anti-Catholicism was on the decline. The Roman Church in the U.S. was on the up, more staunchly ultramontane than Spain. And so it went on the popular front for nearly a decade.

Seeds of skepticism and doubt had been sown. Memories of mass death and plunder hung over a goodly per cent of the male population. The civil rights movement was born. In its infancy it was not wise enough to know the despair of the late 1960's nor strong enough to have concrete promise. Society was changing fast, fast, faster. Trepidation was the fruit flowering in the late 1950's and early 1960's as the seeds from World War II matured and the civil rights advocates began to realize more than a Supreme Court ruling on desegregated schools was needed to achieve justice in democratic America.

Protestants stepped forth first to identify a new mood, one of anxiety, fear and meaningless existence. Growing recourse to psychoanalytical treatment was a major proof-text. Debunking of "positive thinking" as a cure-all set in. Theologians and preachers dragged out the novels of Franz Kafka, Albert Camus, Jean-Paul Sartre; the plays of Arthur Miller and Tennessee Williams; the early poems of T. S. Eliot and the existentialist philosophy of Soren Kierkegaard to illustrate modern man's predicament. How common it was to read or hear about man as "thrown into" existence.

Literature was not the only evidence cited. A few years ago, priests, pastors and seminary professors were a bit slower getting to *Book World* and the *New York Times* magazine than they are today. David Riesman wrote *The Lonely Crowd* in 1953 and William H. Whyte, Jr., published *The Organization Man* in 1956, but it was late in that decade before the views of man in those sociological works had wide impact on the church or theology. Riesman's and Whyte's portrayals of man seeking meaning and stability in social conformity were not less than shocking to churchmen who assumed that such social and emotional needs were satisfied by religion *qua* religion.

The problems of existence became a prime, popular theological focus, along with an increasing admission that persons may indeed find themselves without social, cultural or religious structures on which to fasten existence. Charles D. Kean had said as early as 1947 that a consciousness of the problem of existence as it dominates man and his relation to his situation is the major factor in anxiety.[5] Kean's accuracy became evident as the church became aware of enlarging its focus on the meaning of existence: The church became anxious.

Paul Tillich had, of course, already told the church what was happening. In essays written before he fled Germany in 1933 and in books and articles during the 1950's, the philosopher-theologian probed developments and concepts of the recent past and identified a "search for meaning and the despair of it in the 20th century."[6] According to Tillich, the loss of meaning had long roots extending into medieval bourgeois revolutions which replaced authoritarian structures with reason. A world view based on rational harmony fell under the impact of industrialization and capitalism so that men found themselves at mid-century in a totalitarian structure advertising free enterprise.[7] That is, conformity was demanded while fresh initiative was projected as the ideal. Anxiety is inescapable in this scheme.

Following his theory of correlation in which philosophical interpretation of the objective is given theological response, Tillich posited "the courage to be" as stance for overcoming the threats to existence.[8] Tillich's analysis has not gone without challenge by those who see him as too devoted to dirges, but as the calendar introduced the "soaring sixties" Protestantism was coated with an understanding of man in a muddle of despair. Pascal had summed up the mood nearly 400 years earlier when he wrote in *Pensées:*

When I consider the brief span of my life, swallowed up in the eternity before and behind it, the small space that I fill, or even

see, engulfed in the infinite immensity of spaces which I know
not, and which know not me, I am afraid, and wonder to see
myself here rather than there; for there is no reason why I should
be here rather than there, now rather than then.[9]

Following exactly Kean's analysis of what happens when
the problem of existence becomes prevalent, the church grew
anxious. It had good cause to fear. Obviously, it was not
satisfying the people. Maybe it had not for years? Could the
future be secure? Membership increases slacked, and the year
1962 was a low point for seminary attendance in comparison
to the full-house year of 1957. Protestant church renewal in
the U.S. arose in large measure as a survival tactic. This assertion does not ignore the importance of the theological
work of the Niebuhrs, Tillich, Barth and others. But it
recognizes that the church as institution did not seriously
start thinking about change in structures, liturgies or images
until the institution began to encounter threats.

Among the more serious minds, stress on the meaning
of existence brought a double awareness: of the superficiality
and emptiness of much that the institutional church was doing
and of the sterility of American cultural religion, the worship
of democratic ideas, success and prosperity. Renewal in the
early 1960's, therefore, had a death-wing, those who identified
and proclaimed where the ax should be laid to the stump.
J. A. T. Robinson was its harbinger who put into best-selling
vogue Bultmannian biblical interpretation, Tillichian on-
tology and Bonhoefferian ethics. Three-story universe, an-
thropomorphic God-talk and Christian acquiesence to earthly
principalities and powers did not fit into the recasting of an
"honest to God" mould. Christendom, gone; the "man for
others," in. A spatial God, out; a worldly holiness, with it.[10]
Robinson's *Honest to God* marks a juncture of importance

in modern church history, for it capsuled for the Christian West a number of widespread trends. The sales success of the book indicated that thousands, who could never comprehend the definition of demythologize, were willing to contemplate changes in the received religious patterns and postulations.

The fact that Robinson was a prelate-churchman rather than an academic theologian is significant. It signals the renewal movement's nature as a burst from within. This is not to imply that the bishop's theological forerunners were not churchmen, as indeed they were (or are). But it does mean that at least one bureaucrat was listening to theologians, a phenomenon not altogether common in the 20th century.

One of the first places in-the-world renewal language caught on was in the Protestant campus student movement, long a site of ecumenical cutting edges. The international student initiatives were literally the precursors of modern ecumenism, including the World Council of Churches. In the 1950's there were new twists on old liturgical themes at National Student Christian Federation gatherings. Student demands for implementation of the Supreme Court school de-segregation ruling began to inch into the news. Groups to study theology and the world situation were formed. The next decade brought more defections from lethargy and un-questioning acceptism.

A student at the University of Texas in Austin proclaimed in *motive* magazine in late 1962 that "such terms as 'con-frontation,' 'dialogue,' 'responsibility,' 'involvement,' and 'commitment' are the regular jargon of the campus religious organizations. This new vocabulary has replaced old terms to which many students are immune. Instead of being 'saved,' man is now reconciled; being in 'sin' is estrangement."[11]

The declaration could have been made on other campuses. It now sounds simultaneously familiar and foreign. The list of words are still around, but they do not mean the same thing to students as they did in 1962. They are now the words of establishment religion. With the exception of "confrontation," the dwindling, almost vanished, student wing of the church has a newer vocabulary: happening, caucus, lifestyle, peace and protest.

"Jargon" from the University of Texas in 1962 is no aside in the renewal movement, for in that year the Austin Faith and Life Community under Joseph Mathews was coming into its own. The community was later moved to Chicago and merged with a World Council project to become the Ecumenical Institute, one of the foremost examples of a type of renewal approach.

motive's contributor explained that campus groups like Inter-varsity Christian Fellowship and Campus Crusade for Christ represented a withdrawal from society, an old view of institutions of higher education and outdated attempts to "convert." There was no pleasure in the admission that these old-fashioned Christian approaches—unrenewed—had followers in great number. There was hope. The "moving" student movement was also doing its thing by being "covenanted" and seeing the renewal of a sick society through the church as instrument of social reform.

An interplay, perhaps struggle, between what was represented in the disjuncture between the Faith and Life Community and the Campus Crusade for Christ in Austin in 1962 plots the history of American Protestantism in the 1960's. The liberal, renewing church leaders took the new "jargon." The conservative, status quo churchmen took biblicism. Though not out to "convert" the world, a generation of students set out to save church and society from traditionalism by renewing both. Whatever they accomplished, the students did convert most mainline Protestant churchmen to their terminology.

The fundamentalists, now few, have been relatively silent on a national level in recent years. They can have nothing to say on many social and political issues because they believe in not making religious expressions on such topics. Liberals and fundamentalists both learned in the 1930's that neither can successfully shout down the other. Conservative-to-fundamental Protestants have been searching for a strategy to combat the renewal syndrome. They may have found one in a rapidly expanding "selective giving" campaign which has hit several cities, which proposes to earmark funds only for church work thought fitting. The outcome awaits time. Within all major American Protestant Churches, except the Southern Baptist Convention and the Lutheran Church Missouri Synod, the renewalists have their head, and the Baptist and Lutheran bodies are not without change-seekers.

In 1962, the Campus Crusade for Christ is said to have made such inroads on the basketball team of Rice University that a crisis was reached. The "Christian" crusaders would not pass the ball to the non-crusade "pagans." The situation in the church at large is somewhat reversed at the moment. The renewalists have the ball and intend to dribble a while. Survival seems to require acceptance of their rules.

Catholic Renewal

That Catholic renewal was moved by survival is more difficult to show, since the concern is directly related to the formal gathering of bishops in the Second Vatican Council. Catholic updating appears not to have flowed out of the social context to the extent of Protestant change-making. It would, however, be simplistic to assume that Catholics in the U.S. were unaffected by despair and anxiety just because Protestant theologians rather than archbishops were verbally agonizing over lost man. And it must be imagined that Pope John was aware of the general religious climate in Europe. Perhaps someone at the Vatican even knew of the sociological studies of Gabriel LeBras.

American readers have been reminded that LeBras observed in the 1950's "that a certain railroad station in Paris appears to have a magical quality, for rural migrants seem to be changed from practicing to non-practicing Catholics the very moment they set foot into it."[12] Peter Berger gave the reminder and he also noted, on the basis of sociological study, that *"aggiornamento* usually arises out of tactical considerations."[13] Pope John's motivations, plans and intentions for the Vatican Council are much studied. Conclusions are not easily drawn.

At the beginning of the second session of the Council, Pope Paul explicitly denied that Pope John had convened the prelates "from earthly motives" or "force of circumstances." Pope Paul attributed his predecessor's action to the insight of one "who understood the Divine Will, one who penetrated into the dark and tormented needs of our age."[14] The announcement of the Council came upon the Christian world as such a shock and plans moved so rapidly that little attention to a *why* was possible.

In a radio broadcast in September 1962, Pope John said that two major concerns were the attainment of peace and the establishment of social justice. That his desire for *aggiornamento* aimed at obtaining these goals cannot be discounted. He, like the students at the University of Texas in 1962, wanted to heal a sick society through the instrument of the church. Before attempting the treatment, the pontiff obviously realized that the medical apparatus needed some adjustments.

Also true is Avery Dulles' observation that Vatican II's *Constitution on the Church* begins with the idea of church "as a people to whom God communicates Himself in Love."[15] The Council did not operate in Tillichian fashion, laying out the critical situations and letting theology respond with a satisfying answer. It must be doubted that a Pope presiding over the convocation of the Catholic hierarchy could seriously entertain the possibility that church foundations might quiver and quake. Protestantism can conceive of this happening because the tapestry of its history is filled with the rifts and scars of splits.

Had the likelihood of upheaval as well as renewal been addressed by the Council, the church may better have been able to deal with post-Vatican II developments. Again, Berger has made a pertinent observation. He said that had Catholic authorities been more aware of the sociological conditions, intense shock over contemporary tumbling and tossing would not have been so great.[16]

It is safe to say that Vatican II renewal was essentially aimed at preparing the Church to labor for peace, justice, ecumenical harmony; to do away with formal trappings which caused sluggishness, and to shape it up spiritually, liturgically and structurally for its non-Christendom future in a technological world. If mushrooming *aggiornamento* among laity and young priests and nuns has been disapproved by most of the hierarchy, this does not mean that all interest in renewal has been given up by Pope, curia and bishops. It implies different conceptions of what Christianity should be about.

Insufficient time for misunderstanding had lapsed when the first session of the Council concluded. Pope John still lived. The Ecumenical Protestant Churches, free Orthodoxy and most Catholics were intoxicated with what was happening. Denominational observers from the U.S. came home in a swivit of enthusiasm, almost as though Protestants had never before really believed the church-revitalizing talk they were always using. Assurance levels went up, ever higher.

There was apprehension among Protestants that a successor to Pope John might not continue the Council. The day on which the white smoke over Vatican City gave Giovanni Battista Montini to the world as Paul VI, a Methodist annual conference was meeting in the mountains of Tennessee. Where were the young clergy members? Not listening to the report of the conference committee on history and archives. They were glued to the radio to know whether a conservative or liberal pontiff would emerge. What shouts of joy greeted Montini's name. "The Council will go on."

Vatican II and post-council days are those in which the phrase "church renewal" gained its ascendancy. The term existed previously, mostly in formal theology and in ecumenical and student circles of Protestantism. With Vatican II it left these ghettoes for the headlines. From there it bounced into both the fertile and infertile ground of bureaucracies, meeting syntax and never-ending agendas of problems and challenges.

The years since the Council closed at the end of 1965, so short a time ago, form the period in which most church features defined as renewal have taken on momentum. The scope is breathtakingly large, even in respect to the implementation in Catholicism of Council insights. The process of giving up medieval ways and views has been so speedy that the considerable conservative reaction setting in can hardly be surprising when it is realized that a vernacular liturgy was novelty less than a decade ago. To an old mind, a long distance extends between the *Sanctus* in English and a nun in a mini-skirt.

Changes moving toward more cooperation in inter-church relations are directly linked to the Council. How long it will be before Catholic, Orthodox and Protestant Christians may officially take the Eucharist together remains unknown, but the decision for an ecumenical future has been made. Before the final Vatican II session was four years old, mutual recognition of Protestant and Catholic ministry was reality in Dutch universities, churches' aid to war-blighted Biafra was coordinated on the international level, an (almost) all-Christian conference of churches bloomed in Texas, ecumenical parishes were tried, and a New York congregation of the United Church of Christ scrapped its building and moved in to share a sanctuary maintained by the Catholic Paulist Fathers.

After-1965-years also saw the greatest surge of renewal literature, proposals and case studies, and concrete updating efforts in denominations. Ecumenism, social action, liturgical enlivenment and education reforms have been keystones. Practically every Protestant Church in the nation has overhauled its Christian training materials since 1965. Nine churches have consorted together in the Consultation on Church Union to the point that organic merger or divorce are the only open options. All churches have set some "crisis in the nation" priority, and some have voted enormous funds to push racial justice, ghetto improvement and human self-determination. Rock music, interpretative dance and avant-garde films are likely at any church gathering and in congregations of all traditions.

Sweeping structural reform has been passed or is anticipated by United Methodist, Disciples of Christ, Episcopal, Presbyterian, U.S. and Brethren Churches. Coalitions for evangelism, social action, political pressure and education abound. Added to what has taken place within institutional frameworks are the unspecialized celebration developments such as Corita Kent's religious-secular art, Malcolm Boyd's *Are You Running With Me, Jesus?* prayers, jazz and folk worship and Gertrude Stein set to music at church. These are marketable products to be used by anyone.

Tentative Conclusions

Two tentative conclusions are allowable on the basis of a brief survey of the history of contemporary church renewal. First, the movement began on the outer limits of institutionalized Christianity, moved toward the center, received crowning endorsement in Vatican II and became proclaimed institutional church direction. Second, although renewal's facade is itself many faceted, it is shoring up for onslaughts marshalled by conservatives and revolutionaries.

Proclaiming renewal as institutional Christianity's hope and help is quite in keeping with its traditions. From Pope to democratic assemblies, the Christian Churches have *ex cathedra* consciousness. "Thus sayeth" characterizes most things Christian. The documents of Vatican II were literally pontificated. The many statements on renewal themes issued by World and National Councils of Churches are presented with solemn consensus. Stephen C. Rose subtitled his much-discussed *The Grass Roots Church* with "A Manifesto for Protestant Renewal."[17] When the United Methodist Church was merged into existence in 1968, the first quadrennial banner declared "A New Church for a New Age."

So what is bad about proclaimed renewal? Nothing, unless the proclaimer tries to control the course of the word. Unleashed, any message must go where it will and do what it will. Pope Paul finds himself now in the somewhat strange position of reacting conservatively against forces he helped set loose. No enemy of renewal, the pontiff evidently would like the movement to keep its "proclaimed Vatican II" shape.

Finally, the picture of the church which stands out most clearly is one of mass confusion. Let the picture have some details. In late 1968 the 1.5 million member American Baptist Convention frankly said it contained at least seven identifiable, mostly organized, pressure groups. One was a black caucus, typical now in all integrated churches. Another was women; one, conservatives. Several shaped up along age lines: young, younger and youngest, all thinking none else was doing what the church ought to do in renewing itself to meet late 20th century needs.

A Catholic layman recently explained that renewal had proved so divisive in his parish that he felt more comfortable at the Presbyterian church. He listed four divisions in his home congregations, groups which he said glared at one another during worship. Those over 60 want to pretend the liturgy is still in Latin. Members aged 40 to 60 want things progressive but steady. For the group between 20 and 40, the new is in. Those under 20, the layman said, seem confused by the whole thing and tend to be socially conservative, if a bit unconcerned about the sacrifice of the Mass.

In a Southern city, a Protestant judicatory decided to form a house church in a predominantly black urban renewal neighborhood. A sensitive staff was employed. Attendance was not bad. In fact, the church drew the white dissidents from suburban churches all over town, but had a hard time enlisting anybody from the block.

A once-large metropolitan church in a university-to-hippie community caught renewal fever. It had to do something, for most of the members were old and dying. Most pews were empty on Sundays. The new ministerial direction was toward the young pacifist-minded. There was moderate numerical success, and considerable alteration of furniture and program. Of course, the remaining older members left, many going to a nearby, also renewing, congregation where the stress was on drama and public lectures instead of on peace activities. Plays and speeches can be avoided more easily than psychedelic posters in the vestibule. A lull in the peace movement sent the first church back to committee. The building looks vacant now. But as long as endowment lasts, it will remain, forebodingly planning to renew and survive.

Renewal-consciousness has come to the fore as church self-consciousness. Renewal has been co-opted by the institutional forms of Christianity as a means *and* an end. As self-serving program, renewal is as unwilling to die for humanity or the glory of God as any form of traditionalism. Stephen Rose suggested "abandonment" as the strategy whereby the church relates itself to the world. His proposal was widely accepted, but not without the church falling into the trap Rose warned against. He wrote:

The danger is that anonymous, self-giving abandonment on the part of the Church will reveal itself to be smug, self-righteous, and pompous. Such self-righteousness would . . . reveal itself as a clinging to vestiges of moralism, institutionalism, and cheap grace in the implicit statement, "See how righteous I am! I give without asking in return. I engage in suffering because I will it. I represent a new, relevant religious emphasis."[18]

And that is how the church came to be renewingly unrenewed.

Notes

1 By far the most careful study of the Churches of the Third Reich is that of J. S. Conway, *The Nazi Persecution of the Churches* (New York: Basic Books, Inc., 1968). From captured files, Conway shows the Nazi irritation with Catholic Action, pp. 88ff.

2 Jacques Ellul, "The Situation in Europe," *Man's Disorder and God's Design*, Vol. IV (New York: Harper & Row, 1948), pp. 59-60.

3 Reinhold Niebuhr, "The Situation in the U.S.A.," *ibid.*, p. 80.

4 *Ibid.*, p. 82.

5 Charles D. Kean, *The Meaning of Existence* (New York: Harper & Row, 1947), chap. vi.

6 Paul J. Tillich, *Courage To Be* (New Haven: Yale University Press, 1953), p. 142.

7 *Cf.*, Tillich, "The World Situation," *The Christian Answer*, ed. Henry P. Van Dusen (New York: Charles Scribners Sons, 1954).

8 *Courage To Be, op. cit.*, pp. 171ff.

9 Blaise Pascal, *Pensées*, Section III, "The Necessity of the Wager," Fragment 194.

10 J. A. T. Robinson, *Honest To God* (Philadelphia: The Westminster Press, 1963).

11 Ruth Ann Short, "The Student Movement Moves," *motive* (November 1962), p. 8.

12 Peter L. Berger, *A Rumor of Angels* (Garden City: Doubleday & Company, 1969), p. 40.

13 *Ibid.*, p. 27.

14 Pope Paul VI, Opening Address to the Second Session of the Second Vatican Council (September 29, 1962). *Council Speeches of Vatican II*, eds. Hans Küng, Yves Congar, O.P., and Daniel O'Hanlon, S.J. (Glen Rock, N.J.: Paulist Press, 1964).

15 Avery Dulles, S.J., "The Church," *The Documents of Vatican II*, ed. Walter M. Abbott, S.J. (New York: The America Press, 1966), p. 12.

16 Interview with H. Elliott Wright, January, 1969.

17 Stephen C. Rose, *The Grass Roots Church: A Manifesto for Protestant Renewal* (New York: Holt, Rinehart and Winston, Inc., 1966).

18 *Ibid.*, p. 123.

PART TWO / *Passing Through*

Introduction to Part Two

The declaration that renewal is the church's way of perpetuating its institutional self is tantamount to a blanket charge of hypocrisy. Nothing wanting to be viewed favorably by the public is free of hypocritical tendencies, and church renewal craves love. On top levels, renewal-pushing bureaucrats spend enough on airline tickets and useless consultations per year to feed good-sized communities in Appalachia or the Middle East. Since mission to the hungry is on renewal's agenda, such expenditures are hypocritical, even if ecumenical.

Not all, however, living under an updating religious banner are agents of fluttering self-righteousness. Many of the most creative, gospel-bearing ventures in modern Christianity have stopped, or never began, labeling themselves, "renewal." In order to separate the wheat from the chaff—chaff being the major ingredient in any ecclesiastical bag—concentration on types of renewal is necessary. At this point, the term will be allowed to stand though it does not always apply. Prior to its co-option by the institutions, "renewal" was not the bad word it now is.

The four following chapters deal with renewal types. For detailed descriptions of specific situations or theories, readers are referred to sources listed at the end of this volume. The purpose of this section is to suggest some of re-

71

newal's practical faces and to prepare the ground for thoughts
on options for Christian directions. Interestingly, most of the
types treated confess to the God-following attitude. Discussed
are geographic and congregational experiments, overarching
organizational approaches, institute-sponsored ideologies and
black church initiatives. True to the American policy of
segregation, the latter represents a world of its own, but one
increasingly on the forefront of church deliberations.

Missing are elaborations on the so-called "Catholic revolution" of post-Vatican II years. Several factors dictated the decision to omit the topic. First, Catholic renewal as such is
tightly controlled by the hierarchy and falls almost entirely
into the overarching pattern type. It depicts attempts to implement Vatican II thrusts. The enormous job of evaluating
the Council is grist for many writers and scholars. A recap
here is unnecessary repetition. Moreover, developments are
predictably institutional moves. In John Cardinal Dearden's
late March 1969 innovations in Detroit—unrigid Mass sched-
ules, situational priest garbs and more lay participation—
were promulgated for an entire archdiocese. Rigid enforce-
ment of non-rigidity somehow lacks luster. Vatican II Catholic renewal has never pretended to be anything except
institution-oriented. However, as an example of Catholic updating and its fate, movement not originating in the Council's image will be considered.

Second, "Catholic revolution," as was stated in chapter
one, is more reaction to renewal than part of it, if it is genuine revolution. Phenomena like the "underground church"
will come up after the section on renewal types. Third, Catholic upheaval has been pounded so hard in the press that by
now it is boring to write or read about. A moratorium should
be called on giddy reporting—whether in the *New York*

Times, the *National Catholic Reporter* or *Twin Circles*—which acts as if last week was the first time anything novel happened. The intensive coverage elsewhere of Roman foundation-shaking means it can be passed over quickly here, recognized but hardly swallowed as intoxicant.

4 / Renewal in Your Own Backyard

The hand of the Lord was upon me, and
brought me out by the Spirit of the Lord, and
set me down. . . . (Ezek. 37:1).

At least four models for experimental Christian ministries having a geographic and/or congregational focus exist in the American brew stirred with the renewal stick. There may be more, but those discussed in this chapter have been the most significant. The task at hand is to say what has happened to images of models rather than to present full historical sketches of original experiments themselves. Some comment is essential, of course, on motives, processes and current situations.

The models differ, sometimes greatly, but they share a basic characteristic: they developed in given places and came to claim or be endowed by observers with model-power because of perseverance. Renewal which has sprung from concretely-centered projects must be kept distinct from renewing programs of churches on national or international levels. The specifics came first, in part causing churches to question age-old presuppositions and to talk about change.

However, the models have not remained in isolation, for they have instigated efforts in other localities or spheres and lent their language to the church jargon pool. Models can,

to a degree, be evaluated on the basis of what they produce
or fail to produce as they are championed. The four will be
presented in basic chronological order because of some important interconnections.

*MODEL A: Develop a Christian Community Unfettered by
Inherited Denominational Structures.* In the mid-1940's the
first notable, post-World War II renewal experiment arose in
the U.S., the ecumenical Church of the Saviour in Washington, D.C., which emerged from a small group centered around
Gordon Cosby, an Air Force chaplain of Baptist background.
A first meeting in 1946 led to its formal establishment in
1947. The church has never eschewed cooperation with denominations or delegated ecumenical units. It has simply
managed to circumvent traditional denominationalism by
building from the ground up. The constitution declares:

The Church of the Saviour is to be regarded as part or unit of
Christ's Church, with a distinctive ecumenical spirit and approach, allowing freedom of worship, practice and belief among
its own constituents, while remaining true to the basic values in
the stream of historic evangelical Christianity; attempting to
bear a unique witness of spiritual power, while at the same time
recognizing the validity, the integrity and the rights of self-
determination of all Christian groups and denominations.

Elizabeth O'Connor carefully chronicles the first eight
years of the new approach to Christian *koinonia*, service and
evangelism in *Call to Commitment.*[1] Included were the various missions: Potter's House, the famed coffeehouse; the
Potter's House Workshop; the Dayspring Retreat Center, a
renewal center devoted to the emotionally disturbed, alco-
holic and recently released mental patients, and various other
"kingdom outposts."

A second O'Connor volume, *Journey Inward, Journey Outward*,[2] continues the stories through 1968, detailing changes and new initiatives. To a greater extent than the first, the second book delineates the church's philosophy as one where spiritual introspection within the fold leads to the sharing of gifts in human service. The Church of the Saviour's ventures in worship, community involvement and personal enrichment are impressive, but nothing about the experiment is in proper perspective apart from the theology of church membership.

Miss O'Connor explains that members—who undertake two years of membership training—understand the Christian Church as the gathering of those who are committed to Christ and to one another in the living of a common life. "We are to be pioneers, missionaries, evangelists, teachers, and prophets—representatives of the new humanity."[3] The church is quite serious when it speaks of "covenant relationships" in love and of Christians called to be "saints." But from all indications, it is not easy to be a full member of the Church of the Saviour! Discipline in all things is required out of voluntary commitment, although dogmas are not imposed.

In keeping with St. Paul's observations about "varieties of gifts" in I Corinthians 12, and in honest link with contemporary pluralism, members of the Washington community have wide latitude in determining the mission most suitable to their interests and capabilities. In the spectrum are menial work and personal contacts in the coffeehouse, social rehabilitation, a housing Restoration Corps, education through a Covenant Community or ministry to junior citizens in a "For Love of Children" outreach.

The worship, discipline and study program of the church suggest a sectarian consciousness of pietistic flavor which is not necessarily negative. Anabaptist roots seem blended with service motifs similar to those of the Protestant monks of Taizé, France. Small in numerical strength, the Cosby-led community has had impact disproportionate to size. The simple, fully participatory worship forms have been held up for emulation by churchmen, publications and Christian education materials of many origins. Bridging the gap between clergy and laity provides models for those devoted to revival of the diaconate.

Yet there are problems with the extension of the Church of the Saviour type community throughout the churches precisely because of its sectarian nature. The vocabulary is inspiring, and sectarian language can easily be utilized apart from practical experience. Exactly this has happened to the model. For example, the United Methodist Church is currently trying to implement local church restructuring by employing words and patterns not divorced from objective features of the Church of the Saviour. Provision is made for any number of small group-initiated missions and tasks, expanded community ministry is encouraged, and terms like "servant church," *"koinonia"* and sometimes "covenant" are keystones.

Top level church institutions have co-opted the model language because they cannot afford to take either its structure or its style. Vast connectional systems would collapse should local churches be genuinely urged to follow the example of Mr. Cosby and friends. Appearances of new life need never be more than facades.

Further, it must be observed that little impetus for the form or theology fostered by the Church of the Saviour has poured forth at local levels in major denominations. A survey of 1,318 new Methodist congregations established between 1950 and 1964, two-thirds of them in metropolitan areas, revealed small awareness of the church as pioneer or prophet.

Both the leaders and selected members picked religious education as the church's primary task. "Act as prophetic voice" was fifteenth, the bottom of the list, below "oppose communism." "Service to the needy" was ninth, just under "soul saving." "Maintenance of fellowship and discipline" came second, but the stress must fall on "maintenance." Innovation moving away from tradition was not implied. Third in importance was the providing of spiritual care, guidance and growth for members. Stand-taking on social issues was twelfth.[4]

Sectarian Christianity, even when absolutely comparable to *the* gospel, gnaws at the institutional church's livelihood. It did at Carthage in the second century, in Bohemia in the 15th century, at Wittenberg in the 16th, in England in the 18th and at Rome, Geneva or Nashville, Tennessee, in the 20th. The institutions have found new verbal life in the Church of the Saviour model, but hardly more.

Such conclusion does not prejudice the witness or work of the model itself. There is room, however, to doubt the applicability of the piety of the Church of the Saviour to society in general. The church has remained open to outsiders, a remarkable feat since it has a classical evangelical base which historically has tended to edge toward spiritual pridefulness. Taken out of its original context, the model assumes the self-righteousness now rampant in the updating stances of institutional Christianity.

Miss O'Connor implies in *Call to Commitment* that all Christian groups can move into a new land where structures are servants rather than masters. She is probably correct, but a will to risk a period of flexibility and perhaps failure is required. Most denominations and their congregations have no such will. Were there more actual pioneers, the style as well as the vocabulary of the Church of the Saviour might define the Christian future. But the world has few frontiersmen. Given the fact that the traditional churches continue to domi-nate the religious scene, the full weight of the model will not be adopted. More creditable are the experiments which Rose-mary Ruether calls "communities which retain a certain re-lationship to traditional structures but which are still free to form their own life and to define their own relationship to those structures."[5]

In making appeal for Christian communities to counteract institutionalism, Mrs. Ruether, who is a sort of Pentecostal Roman Catholic, cited two Protestant experiments in Wash-ington, D.C., neither of them the Church of the Saviour. The omission could have been inadvertent, or because the church has been so much studied, or because she had no firsthand experience with it. Still, the fact of its prominence would suggest its inclusion in Mrs. Ruether's most serious quest for fresh wineskins. The two Washington churches, the Church of St. Stephen and the Incarnation (Episcopal) and the Com-munity of Christ (American Lutheran) bear some marks of similarity to their elder neighbor in inner-city District of Columbia. A major distinction is denominational vs. non-denominational affiliation. Even the non-hierarchy-heeding Mrs. Ruether is not prone to urge back-turning on institu-tional structures. Freedom, she asks, but with a lifeline.

Skeptical, yes—the truth is that the renewal model which builds from the ground up will not sail on the present ecclesi-astical and theological sea.

MODEL B: Urban Colonization. Inner-city ministry experi-ments have some nuances of building from the ground up, but they normally utilize existing church facilities and groups as foundation stones, whether they focus on poverty situations or middle class apartment complexes. They also may be less theologically acute than the Church of the Saviour. U.S. cities are crammed full of experimental church projects. Some few have arisen within communities to meet special challenges but most have been set in from the outside. Once established, the efforts can have firm community bases or become imperialistic.

The model for almost all modern urban church work, A-1 in renewal priorities, is the East Harlem Protestant Parish in New York. One of the most studied happenings of the 20th century religious scene, the parish has influenced Protestant and Catholic programs. The story is romantic, hard-nosed, painful, beautiful and much told. East Harlem Protestant Parish (EHPP) was born in 1948 out of the determination of three young ministers, Donald Benedict, Archie Hargraves and George William (Bill) Webber to bring Christian witness and compassion to what was then and is now one of the nation's worst slums, a geographically defined upper Manhattan area peopled primarily by Negroes and Puerto Ricans.

With meager financial support from four denominational boards of missions and the New York City Mission Society, and armed with enormous supplies of willpower, the young men opened a storefront church. The drudgery of overcoming community apathy, fighting housing neglect and dirty politics, forming ties with street gangs, opposing the narcotics trade and reflecting a spirit of Christian love had moderate success. Time passed. Other storefront churches were opened; a group ministry emerged; medical personnel, social workers, lawyers and scores of seminarians, most from Union Theological, came to join. Narcotics rehabilitation became a primary commitment, leading to the establishment in 1965 of Exodus House as an independent institution.

Benedict and Hargraves moved in the early 1950's to Chicago where an EHPP type project was set up on the West

Side. Now with the Community Renewal Society, Benedict had a hand in shaping inner-city projects in a number of cities. Bill Webber, whose writings evidence the influence of George McLeod's Iona Community in Scotland and the mission theology of Ceylonese Methodist D. T. Niles, was left as the leader and interpreter of the original model. Such luminaries as attorney William Stringfellow and mission expert Letty Russell were later to be closely linked with the parish. Webber has been number one spokesman, laying out the first two stages of the parish history in *God's Colony in Man's World*[6] and *The Congregation in Mission.*[7]

More was involved than spiritual ministry among and social service for the residents of overcrowded East Harlem. Webber explains there was a unifying ingredient within the staff which was bound by a common discipline and budget. At the early stage, the idea was to bring the members of the parish into the *koinonia* of the discipline. Indeed, the experiment was a colony come in from the outside with a mission. Within the ghetto mood of today, this colonizing would undoubtedly be viewed as paternalistic. It was then, also, but not so obviously. Still, there were turbulent days.

Grafting ghetto residents onto the disciplined community was not easy. A second stage outlook is reflected in Webber's title, *The Congregation in Mission*. There was still a unified approach, a cohesive staff-centered program, but there was, in up-to-date terms, a degree of decentralization. Some unhappy staff times marked the late fifties, one a fifteen-month period when William Stringfellow was at theological loggerheads with compatriots. The Episcopal lay theologian later wrote about his uneasiness:

The Church is much tempted by conformity to the world, by accommodating the message and mission to the particular society in which the Church happens to be . . . instead of honoring the integrity of the Gospel for all societies and for all sorts and conditions of men in all times and places. This temptation beguiled the group ministry of the East Harlem Protestant Parish. They plunged into all sorts of social work and social action. . . . It was, in many ways, an admirable, if idealistic, and, in Christian terms, naive effort. But they neglected and postponed the proclamation and celebration of the Gospel in East Harlem. In the congregations of the parish, the Bible was closed; in the group ministry there was even scorn for the Bible as a means through which the Word of God is communicated in contemporary society. . . . The parish—and especially the group ministry—was becoming dependent . . . upon its "good works," rather than upon the Gospel, as such, for its justification.

In such circumstances, the hostility of the group ministry toward the Church outside East Harlem, and, indeed, toward other Churches within East Harlem unaffiliated with the parish . . . became more arrogant and proud. . . . One of the clergy in the group ministry blandly explained that the Church outside East Harlem was dead and that the East Harlem Protestant Parish represented the "New Jerusalem" . . . of American Protestantism, the example through which American Protestantism would be purified and renewed.[8]

Mr. Stringfellow did not declare that the entire course of EHPP history fitted into this pattern, and he noted the rethinking of the purpose taking place when he departed in late 1957. His criticism may be too strong, but there was a time in the late 1950's and early 1960's when Union Theological students doing field work in East Harlem seemed to consider as excluded from the kingdom classmates not innerurbanly occupied.

An unfortunate chapter in the East Harlem impact is that it was the era of intensively colonizing social action which has been bled into the denominations' renewing streams. Not

until the early 1960's did the East Harlem literature pour
forth, most of it depicting an earlier period in the experiment. The literature of urban ministry now reads with the
same fervor for action which the brilliant Mr. Stringfellow
found least Gospel-bearing in East Harlem.

Moreover, it might come as shock to many churchmen to
learn that EHPP is no longer in the "colony" or "congregation in mission" stages, phrases that appear ad nauseam in
ecclesiastical promotional pieces. Said a recent General Assembly of the Presbyterian Church, U.S. (Southern): "To
accommodate the diversity of structures in modern society,
new colonies of the church of Christ must be formed. These
'para congregations,' as they might be called, would not take
the place of existing local parish churches. They could be in
shopping centers, on university campuses, in industrial complexes, in apartment buildings, in office buildings, or among
vocational groups."[9] And a report to the General Assembly of
the United Presbyterian Church declared: "Extension of
ministry requires a readiness to act immediately whenever a
need becomes obvious." The immediately preceding paragraph defined extension as "horizontal movement of congregations and judicatories expressing their concern for the
world outside of their 'normal' structural life."[10]

George Webber is now gone from EHPP, first giving his
energies to the ecumenical Metropolitan Urban Service
Training (MUST I) and more recently accepting the presidency of New York Theological Seminary. Partly because of
staff disagreements, but more because of the changing nature
of the ghetto, EHPP is now little more than a skeleton hover-
ing over a group of independent agencies. Non-covenanted
pluralism seems to have won. The colony withdrew. Two
family churches with a five-minister team came under the
parish board, along with a unit called "permanent availabil-

ity," which provides central services and clinic, and a number of task forces concerned with mental health, education and cultural activities.

Related are Exodus House, MUST I, a credit union, a housing program called Metro North, a local council of churches, the storefront Church of the Living Hope and certain government-funded enterprises. Also in the consortium is Emmaus House, a facility which merits separate attention later. The seminarians are mostly gone. John C. Bennett, Union's leading light, has said that the frontier for the theological student is now the suburb. The implication is that the ghetto does not want, or does not need, the colonizer. Few persons ask anymore what is going on at EHPP. The model has been lost to the co-opting institutions in dire need of innovating props, even if they are a quarter-century old.

The suggestion made here is not that the parish was a failure. The observation is that the churches are not well served in urban ministries to co-opt a romanticized image of a model while failing to co-opt the problems which go along with it. Carving a colony of God in the world is damned hard, as anyone associated with EHPP might testify. The chance that social action is clouding the church's vision—Stringfellow's contention about the parish at one point—is underscored by Peter Berger:

It seems to me as a Christian one must have a concern for the woes of mankind, to be involved in a moral imperative. . . . The one thing that troubles me is that social action or social engagement can be a convenient method of avoiding contact with the question of truth in religion. . . . I'm not, of course, opposed to social action. It's as if a man has trouble with his wife and then goes out and fights for civil rights. That may be of great help to civil rights, but it has nothing to do with his relationship with his wife. . . .[11]

Colonizing with a social knife or colonizing of any kind may be the wrong approach to a church renewing, human renewing urban ministry. Take as example one less grandiose in scope than EHPP, the apartment house ministry. This is essentially a colonizing process.

In the renewal boom about 1965, ministries in high rise dwellings came on big. Recipients of attention were members of the mobile middle class instead of slum inhabitants, but the motivation was not vastly different from service to the poor. Something missing was to be provided. Apartment people needed community. Guiding considerations in formulating the experiments were respect for the style of apartment living, a need for reconciliation among neighbors and the development of groups around common interests.[12] Surprisingly, the impetus was not to get persons into sanctuaries around the corner so much as to make the presence of the church felt. Small colonies within the buildings, at least an apartment adaptable to a young clergyman and his family, were often launch agents.

Apartment house ministries continue. They have fared rather badly. Two years after the elevator ascended, Grace Ann Goodman declared the experiments at value's end. Why? Miss Goodman, whose wide experience with church things qualifies her to pass a dictum, said there were two hang ups: "False categorization and outdated operating assumptions."[13] Among the assumptions she cited were beliefs that the type of residence shapes life styles and that "everybody ought to be related to neighborhood concerns and institutions such as churches."[14]

These assumptions were unrealistic, according to Miss Goodman, because for mobile persons housing is an accessory to living, not a framework; apartments are not good places for contacts, and apartment dwellers usually feel no ties to the neighborhood. Her conclusion was that some "churchmen must get over their preoccupation with housing style and get on with helping people deal with the real problems of urban life —the responsible, fulfilling use of their new freedom."[15]

The same can be said for any colonizing attempt. Insofar as the colony model of renewing urban ministry has been taken over by the church's institutions, an outdated model is grasped. The church wants to "do something" for people. Does the church want to "do something" or does it want "something to do"? Activity prolongs life.

MODEL B: Emmaus House, Something All Its Own, Maybe.[1]
Emmaus House is in East Harlem. It cooperates with EHPP. It is a colony of sorts since it came into the ghetto in 1966 rather than being produced there. But the Emmaus center is different from early EHPP. The drive is not to organize satellite churches. Social action is more responsive than initiatory. Emmaus people seem to know Manhattan is a whole island, one connected to the rest of the world. *Being* the church looms as large as developing or renewing the church. A small resident group is supplemented by scattered members for discussion, agape meals, other worship and service. Visitors are frequent. An early church consciousness pervades, reflected in selection of the name from the Emmaus walk and meal of Luke 24. Off Manhattan is Emmaus-on-the-Road retreat center.

Emmaus House came about through Father David Kirk, who has described himself as out of Dorothy Day's *Catholic Worker* movement,[16] and Lyle Young, an Episcopal clergyman. Kirk, a priest of the Melkite Byzantine Rite of Catholicism, is coordinator. Ecclesiastically, the experiment was authorized by the Melkite Rite. Thoroughly ecumenical and

identified with the "new left" in early days, Emmaus House
would undoubtedly never have happened or not lasted long
had the Roman Catholic Archdiocese of New York held
jurisdiction in the matter.

The center identifies with Shalom in the Netherlands, an
agape-eating, Rome-ignoring group dedicated to peace, celebration of God's grace and non-dogmatic Christian confession. Letty Russell, formerly of EHPP, is a participant in
Emmaus House. She has noted the hope for growth "in our
country as Shalom has grown in the Netherlands finding its
support at the grass roots level. Even as our movement takes
shape, we have hopes of completing affiliation with Shalom so
that ours may be a national expression on behalf of world
Christian unity."[17]

For several years, Emmaus was lumped with the "underground church." Indeed, it appeared to many as epitome of
the non-institutional with its "house church" complexion,
unpapally blessed Agape-Masses and freewheeling publication, *The Bread is Rising*. (The title is taken from a whis-
pered hope of peasants in the French Revolution.) Kirk wrote
an account of the community in the Malcolm Boyd-edited
volume, *The Underground Church*.[18]

A *New Yorker* piece in early 1969 was a catalyst for Emmaus reaction against its reputation as a gung-ho "happening"
haven. Martin Marty described the article as "David Underground versus Goliath Establishment; snippy renewalists
versus puffy bishops; neurotic-but-free experiments versus
somnolent Above-grounders."[19] He also quoted from a Kirk
letter stating that Emmaus was more than "naive talk about
revolution, Corita-life-style (or) conversation which reads
like an evening with Malcolm Boyd. . . . We cannot see ourselves associated with the so-called 'Underground church'
movement as it is presently today."[20]

Marty's suggestion that more love and some patience has been mixed in Emmaus' "love-hate relation"[21] with the unreformed church is apparently true. Earlier eschewed denominationalism and institutional ecumenism have not been embraced, but a tendency toward greater charity for the church, or a church, is detectable. This may have been incipient all along, overshadowed by an initially giddy press and religious faddism. In 1968 Letty Russell, writing about Emmaus-projected groups, said that such fellowship "is not designed to conflict with the denominational or confessional affiliation of its members. Rather, it is designed to seek ways beyond the present structures to live and work as one in Jesus Christ . . . all in each place."[22]

Chances are that Emmaus will turn out to be more renewalist than revolutionist in its search for a contemporary Christian life-style. Its future may be very bright, though Emmaus is not currently the model the churches are looking for, especially not in official Catholicism after the Easter, 1969, rant of Pope Paul against the schismatics. Abolishing the red hats of cardinals is enough renewal for many Catholics and Protestants. Emmaus House might do more for humanity and the gospel to go back, or to start, battling with bishops!

MODEL C: Industrial Mission. In 1944, the same year the Taizé community was formed as a secular-work-based effort to unite Christianity, the now Anglican Bishop E. R. Wickham went to the heavily industrial city of Sheffield, England, to launch a truly new project. In the words of one who knows the work, Wickham's industrial mission hoped to bridge the "yawning chasm between thriving industry and the feeble churches. Believing that new strategy and a radical reinterpretation of the Christian faith were imperative, he did not try to bring workers into the church but rather met them on their own industrial ground. Nor did the mission attempt to preach the gospel in traditional terms, but rather listened to the voices in industry and tried through free-for-all discussion to discover arresting and appropriate ways to understand the purposes of God for industrial life."[23]

The first part of this description, incidentally, fits what John Wesley had done in England two centuries earlier. Wickham still deserves a pioneer's tribute. A field left fallow for 200 years is nearly as difficult to clear as it was the first time.

In 1956 the model was begun in the U.S. Detroit was the place. Hugh White was founder, joined the following year by Scott I. Paradise who was fresh from the Sheffield experiment. Paradise is the most visible figure on the industrial mission scene. He has since 1964 headed a project in Boston. There are some fourteen missions functioning.

Initiating motive for the Detroit Industrial Mission (DIM) was need for a "new structure of the church that could work full time on the problems of relating the meaning of faith to the work place."[24] There were two foci: to keep church leaders on local and denominational levels informed about the industrial sphere and to seek engagement with industrial personnel. Contact was first sought through four Episcopal churches in Detroit called, for DIM purposes, the associated parishes. A research orientation gave way to a dialogue-centered program encouraging reflection and self-understanding in church and industry. The ideal was to have a two-way street between the local churches and the factories. Renewal of the church by way of this new involvement was as much a goal as service to the "organization man" manager or the con-formity-ensnared assembly line man. A commanding hope was the desire to urge congregations toward acceptance of a new life-style.

On the church side, DIM failed. A 1968 report from Mission staff members implies that from the beginning there was a turning away from parish association to more direct engagement with persons in industry.[25] Paradise suggests the struggle to be related to local congregations was arduous and long.[26] The parish associations were discontinued in 1960, and the work, which had gained Episcopal, Presbyterian, Methodist and United Church of Christ backing, continued along other lines.

Paradise has explained that the best programs in the parish-related chapter were those of limited objectives like sermon discussion groups, meetings with unemployed and industrial study groups with businessmen. He says, "These programs flourished only with a tremendous investment of time and energy. . . . But instead of reorienting the life of the parish as we had hoped, they seemed rather to add new programs which left the parish basically unchanged. . . ."[27] It is his conclusion that nothing of enduring value happened in the four years of the parish association and "probably renewal of the churches along the lines of our hopes was simply not in the cards."[28]

The Boston Industrial Mission has denominational sponsors but not formal organization or parish tie-ins, undoubtedly because of the failure of the two-way church-industry street in Detroit. The Boston constituency is from the burgeoning scientific-technological community massed around the universities at the mouth of the Charles River. Through informal contacts and voluntary task groups, concern's eye is on personal and corporate responsibility, the social obligations of science and the enhancement of life in the technological age.

Back in Detroit, DIM has emerged as agent of change, evaluator of directors for change and advocate of participation by the industrially employed in life and work. In the wake of the 1967 urban riots, it has taken on community dimensions. DIM has dropped staff-led vocational courses in churches in favor of sessions in which laymen and local pastors are trained to conduct vocational discussions. A report in 1968 said: "The staff's goal at this time is to be a resource to the local church, not to provide the leadership for ongoing church groups. Instead, the Mission feels that it can contribute most to the vitality and renewal of the church by being an active and creative embodiment of the church's mission within industrial structures and the community."[29]

Essentially, the industrial missions in Detroit and Boston have given up church renewal as commonly conceived. The experiment in Detroit was concrete enough, long enough, to test the intentions of traditional parishes. The will was not renewal along DIM lines. Paradise noted that few persons are anxious to challenge the claim that the church exists for the world, though characteristically the assertion is followed by " 'but . . . in order to serve the world the church must . . . be strong itself.' And this opens the door wide for absorption in self-serving activities, cautious protectiveness, and drives for denominational aggrandizement."[30] He echoes William Stringfellow's point that the church's urban work is built on the premise that the church must be rich to minister to the poor.[31] The observation is the same even if industrial and poverty situations are different.

Funds for the Detroit and Boston industrial missions have come from denominational pockets, but one must seriously wonder if national Protestant structures or congregations could or would affirm the models of ministry provided by the maturing projects. The latter-day styles are extra-institutional, basic threats to the structural overhanging of the churches. A really adequate ministry to industry—which is most of the nation—might entail the abolition for financial reasons of traditional parishes which only half-minister to non-industry. It is not, therefore, surprising that the language of the first stage of DIM, the two-way street between plant and church, rolls from the lips of churches wishing to cross boundaries between church and world.

Practically no widespread attention has been given to ministries essentially separated from established parish or community forms. The vocabulary for "new mission" among all mainline churches in the U.S. is so similar that not a pragmatic reason exists for denominations, Roman or Reformation, to remain independent. The statements of realization are beautifully sensitive, passionately open until a last section is reached. That section is a jumble of judicatories, councils, hierarchies, committees, structures and Geneva-come-lately-by-way-of-Rome sputtering. The risk is not yet.

Where there is cognizance that church may have to lose its life, there is equally firm conviction that if there is willingness to lose—for the church not necessary for mankind—then life will be found. Ignored is the fact that Jesus' statement about losing and finding was addressed to persons rather than institutions.

"Extension of ministry," such as into industry, is a life-extending device in most ecclesiastical jargon. The church cannot use the outcome of the industrial missions it set up. A United Presbyterian committee was right when it said: "Our experience to date indicates that 'renewal' is an amorphous word used to describe everything or nothing. 'Extension of ministry,' with certain encouraging exceptions, usually means timid forays of the church from a secure and well-protected base. Survival goals prevail and mission goals are frequently misunderstood or resisted."[32] It was a courageous group which penned that conclusion.

The industrial mission model began as church renewal but

was forced to move to a person and group-centered consciousness apart from traditional churchiness, renewing or not. Acceptance for extensive implementation of its non-parish form
strikes at the very base of institutionalized denominationalism or ecumenism. One wonders if the United Presbyte-
rians are even inspired to forage as far as the model might
lead. Perhaps only a cynic would wish to see an entire General Assembly deployed for the sake of the Word made Flesh.
Still . . .

MODEL D: Traditional Congregation Revamp. By far the
best known and the most common form of church renewal
turns on labors to rejuvenate existing, inherited congregations. This goal is a foremost plank in the platforms of Catholic and Protestant *aggiornamento.* Earliest implementations
of Vatican II decisions gave parishes vernacular liturgies, increasing lay participation and greater urges toward social involvement. Protestant denomination restructures harken
attention to the local scenes. Preliminary organic ideology of
the Consultation on Church Union, the counciliary unit
plotting union of nine Protestant Churches, is parish-cen-
tered.

As in the case of other models of geographic updating,
congregational renewal began locally before it became
churchwide programming. The first experiments were Protestant, and clues were at times taken from the Church of the
Saviour and East Harlem Protestant Parish. Some have sought
inspiration from institute-based renewal approaches discussed
in a later chapter. Independent factors and specific leaders
have been frequent catalysts.

Historically, Judson Memorial Church in New York's
Greenwich Village was the first widely hailed adventure in
established church experimentation with new forms of wor-

ship, mission and congregation consciousness. Under the pastoral leadership of the late Robert Spike from 1949 to 1954, the church, named for Baptist foreign mission founder Adoniram Judson, sought interdenominational status. And it set about to minister to one of the most transitory, youth-inhabited neighborhoods in the world. Since the mid-1950's, Howard Moody and his staff have continued the easygoing but serious work of being the church present and available. Currently, programs in creative arts and work with runaway youths are most evident at Judson, but there is nothing rigid about the approach. A decade or more ago, attempts to reach street gangs were a priority. Judson has remarkably avoided intransigence, a factor partially attributable to the loose membership setup. There is a sustaining nucleus of the committed, but member-making is no Judson preoccupation. Those who come are taken into church and group activities minus formal indoctrination.

The flexibility across the years can be existentially documented with reference to Judson Sunday worship. In the Spike era a formal and aesthetically pleasing liturgy, the kind the avant-garde of the 1950's liked, was standard. It has been replaced by the most informal pattern, conducted in a pewless and pulpitless sanctuary. Drama, dance or film are not outlanders on Sunday mornings. Typically, the service resembles the Sunday School opening exercise at Southern Baptist churches in rural North Alabama. Nobody worries if a prepared order must be altered. There are no carnationed, military-stepping ushers to receive the offering. People smile and greet each other. The clock is not watched. Food in the rear of the sanctuary after the benediction is not sacrilege. Anyone present is given opportunity to say whatever might be on heart or mind, just as anybody at Sunday School opening can interrupt the deacon to make a point. Only it is

unfair to say Judson has borrowed from Southern Sunday
Schools. The style is that produced by the need of urban
anomies to make contacts. If a style suitable for urban Christian worship happens to be the same as the rural South, that
is the problem of Harvey Cox and the sociologists.

Judson's experiment need not be extended. Mention is
made because of its priority and because, in light of familiar-
ity, it is necessary to note that the Greenwich Village church
has not been much copied. Slightly comparable situations do
exist: St. Clement's (Episcopal) outreach to the theatrical district in New York, Brooklyn's Spencer Memorial Presbyterian, the jazz ministry interest of St. Peter's Lutheran in New
York, and parts of the programs at Glide Memorial (Methodist) in San Francisco and First Presbyterian in Chicago's
Woodlawn section.

The model for congregation change emerging from Judson
takes a rather specialized setting. Moreover, it is too uninstitu-
tional to appeal to model selecting bureaucrats whose jobs
depend on standardized benevolence giving.

There are too many situations—some shortlived and others
continuing—of congregation experimentation to cite even a
representative sample. The spectrum extends from denominational "larger parishes" in the lake region of the Cumber-
land Plateau to an embryonic ecumenical congregation in
Burlington, Vermont; from ethnic work at St. Mark's in the
Bowery, New York, to racial reconciliation through St. An-
drew's Presbyterian in suburban Marin City, California.

Of most significant proportions among local church revamps coming before renewal's skyrocket is First United
Methodist Church, Germantown, Pennsylvania, a Philadelphia suburb filled with affluence and poverty. And developments there have been experience as well as experiment.
Guiding influences in the Germantown story are copastors

Robert Raines and Theodore W. Loder. Raines is the most published and the minister nationally known, but he is quick to point out that he is not the "boss" and that the senior level pastorate is decidedly shared. Still the personal importance of the son of retired Bishop Richard Raines of Indianapolis cannot be minimized.

Raines came to Germantown in 1961 from Aldersgate Methodist in Cleveland, the city where Don Benedict, a founder of East Harlem Protestant Parish, spent some time with an inner-city Protestant Parish in the 1950's. Raines' 1961 book, *New Life in the Church*,[33] reflects appreciation for the intensive group study and "house church" approach fostered by the Cleveland parish. Regardless of degree of influence, Raines' stress on discipline and *koinonia* strategy is similar to that associated with the East Harlem Protestant Parish heritage.

He was also in close touch with Gordon Cosby of the Church of the Saviour during, and after, the Cleveland post. But the Raines focus has been different from inner-city colonies or from ground-up congregations. His efforts have been to extend, hone, clarify or adapt frameworks, facilities and manpower found in the highly structured local Methodist church.

In Germantown, Raines found a situation right off the drum of the great American urban mimeograph machine: the neighborhood was in transition, blacks were moving into a formerly all white area, church membership was declining and an enormous building was lapping up funds. A first decision under Raines' leadership was to maintain the church where it is rather than move farther out into Waspville.

Mission and ministry to a racially mixed community meant increasing social action. Some members objected to this, and also to the introduction of dialogue between religion and

politics and to study of the "new theologies" entering the ecclesiastical picture. An honest critique of the dilemma is
given by Raines in *The Secular Congregation*.[34] That book
also presents a detailed account of the Germantown programs
and theology.

Contrary to the short-term membership training class
which has been traditional in 20th century American Methodism, new Germantown members have a mandatory six-week
"Christian Faith and Life Seminar." A second stage is participation in a *koinonia* group lasting approximately one
year. The second is optional but highly recommended. The
church is amazingly alive.

Grounded in a biblical faith which seeks to mediate between what Raines calls the "Priest-secularist controversy,"[35]
the theology of membership has three foci: "come," the welcome of persons into the congregation; "go," service in the
world; and "stay," the backbone structure which must be constantly invigorated by the "come" and "go."[36] In this context
is understood the Raines' phrase "the congregation without
walls." Not only does this mean no Christian community
hiding itself and no locks on the chapel door. It also means
no cleavages among coming, going and staying. It means no
denominational, racial, economic or cultural barriers between neighbors.

Covenant—secular covenant which binds persons together
in worship, work and study—is a key concept at Germantown.
Covenant groups are encouraged for those who desire them.
Out of one group came the Philadelphia Covenant House in
South Germantown, now an independent health, education
and recreation facility receiving wide ecumenical and private
support. It operates in relation to a community council,
hoping to overcome any vestiges of paternalism which may
have first been inherent.

The Germantown staff is drivingly ecumenical, engaged in urban causes, in an Ecumenical Institute sponsored by the Religious Council of the community and the Wellsprings Ecumenical Center which concentrates on church and metropolitan renewal. The church has not recouped its membership losses. (It dropped from nearly 2,000 in 1950 to 1,150 in 1967). No attempt is made to graft onto the roll every person touched by a clergyman, a mission group or a special project. Innovations with the Sunday morning worship services have moved slowly. Raines agrees that finding a worship form which is meaningful to a congregation of diverse individuals is one of the most difficult tasks. The temptation to proliferate services for those with special worship interests has been withstood. Leaders feel that worship is one point where a congregation can be united. They opt for increasing variety in the regular schedule, realizing some groups of constituents may not be comfortable, rather than compartmentalized worship.

Germantown's strides have, for the most part, been made alone so far as denominational ties are concerned. It is well known that now retired Bishop Fred P. Corson of Philadelphia did not, between 1961 and 1968, react favorably to updating at what has been called "a Cathedral of Methodism." Other conference and district officials have usually taken a "hands off" stance. American Methodism had within its fold for a decade (counting Raines' experiences in Cleveland and Germantown) the makings of one of the most forward-looking renewal models imaginable. It, like the other churches, chose not to look until the ecclesiastical chips began to fall.

Not until after men like Gibson Winter and Peter Berger were heard—and the hearing came after the saying—wondering if traditional parishes could ever be renewed did the Protestant Churches get on the renewing bandwagon. This hearing took place along with the shaking provided by Vatican II, a demonstration that tired old Catholicism might not be entirely dead as most Protestants thought prior to 1962.

The assertion prejudices the following chapter, but the case is that three-fourths of everything the United Methodist Church and its forebearer, The Methodist Church, have written about renewal since 1967 is wasted paper. It had a model at Germantown, a style pliably adaptable for practically any local situation. True to denominational thinking, it seemed necessary to renew all levels of the structure instead of concentrating on local congregations where the people live. If mission-active units of men and women need overarching hookups, they will be capable of molding fitting hooks.

United Methodism has officially adopted Germantown language, probably without realizing the toilsome labor which went into development of the reality behind that language, without appreciating the amount of unnecessary ecclesiastical baggage which was permanently stored. Germantown started renewal while there was still time. Now that the time of crisis is hourly cried, it does not have to go purchase oil for its lamps. The word "renewal" has lessened in vocabulary frequency. In a conversation about this volume, Raines remarked, in effect, that he was of the impression "renewal" was a used up word.

None claim that Germantown has reached perfection. It is not minus problems. Yet it is not teasing itself with words. As much as any to be found, the church is doing the work and reaping the joy of the gospel—without singing an anthem to itself. Germantown is probably no good as a church renewal model because it is too unselfconscious, too uninterested in self-preservation.

Notes

[1] Elizabeth O'Connor, *Call to Commitment* (New York: Harper & Row, 1963).

[2] O'Connor, *Journey Inward, Journey Outward* (New York: Harper & Row, 1968).

[3] *Op. cit.*, p. 23.

[4] *A Study of New Church Development, 1967,* carried out by Earl D. C. Brewer, with the assistance of Marie Townsend, through the Religious Research Center, Candler School of Theology, Emory University, Atlanta, Georgia. Sponsored by the Department of New Church Development, Section of Church Extension, the National Division of the Methodist Board of Missions, p. 51.

[5] Rosemary Ruether, "New Wine, Maybe New Wineskins, for the Church," *The Christian Century* (April 2, 1969), p. 447.

[6] George W. Webber, *God's Colony in Man's World* (Nashville: Abingdon Press, 1960).

[7] Webber, *The Congregation in Mission* (Nashville: Abingdon Press, 1964).

[8] William Stringfellow, *My People Is the Enemy* (New York: Holt, Rinehart and Winston, 1964), pp. 88-89.

[9] From a report adopted by the 107th (1968) General Assembly of the Presbyterian Church in the United States. Cited in *Church in Mission* (January 1969), p. 2.

[10] Final report on "Renewal and Extension of the Church's Ministry in the World" from a committee to the 1968 General Assembly of the United Presbyterian Church.

[11] "What's Ahead for the Church?" *World Outlook* (April 1969), p. 9, from an interview with Peter L. Berger.

[12] David C. Rich, "Ministry in High-Rise Apartments," *The Church Creative*, eds. M. Edward Clark, William L. Malconson and Warren Lane Molton (Nashville: Abingdon Press, 1967), pp. 169-177.

[13] Grace Ann Goodman, "End of the 'Apartment House Ministry,'" *The Christian Century* (May 10, 1967), p. 615.

[14] *Ibid.*

[15] *Ibid.*, p. 617.

[16] David Kirk, "Emmaus: A Venture in Community and Communica-

tion," *The Underground Church,* ed. Malcolm Boyd (New York: Sheed & Ward, 1968), p. 139.

[17] Letty Russell, "Emmaus, Agape and Action," *The Bread is Rising* (Winter/Spring 1968), p. 40.

[18] Kirk, *op. cit.*

[19] Martin E. Marty, "A New Sun Shines Down on the Real Emmaus House," *The National Catholic Reporter* (March 19, 1969), p. 10.

[20] *Ibid.*

[21] *Ibid.*

[22] Russell, *op. cit.*

[23] Scott I. Paradise, *Detroit Industrial Mission: A Personal Narrative* (New York: Harper & Row, 1968), pp. xiii-xiv.

[24] Robert W. Terry, "Detroit Industrial Mission, Its Changing Identity," *Church in Metropolis* (Spring 1968), p. 12. Reprinted from *Life & Work* (December 1967).

[25] *Ibid.*

[26] Paradise, *op. cit.,* pp. 97ff.

[27] *Ibid.,* p. 105.

[28] *Ibid.,* p. 112.

[29] Terry, *op. cit.,* p. 14.

[30] Paradise, *op. cit.,* p. 111.

[31] Stringfellow, *op. cit.,* p. 99.

[32] United Presbyterian "Renewal and Extension" report. *Op. cit.*

[33] Robert A. Raines, *New Life in the Church* (New York: Harper & Row, 1961).

[34] Raines, *The Secular Congregation* (New York: Harper & Row, 1968).

[35] *Ibid.,* pp. 3ff.

[36] *Ibid.,* pp. 82ff.

5 / Renewal from "Out There"

Prophesy to the breath, prophesy, son of man . . .
(Ezek. 37:9).

Church renewal plans originating from hierarchical decisions, denominational convention votes and voluntary organization proposals are each in some way intended for local congregation betterment as well as for universal structure revitalizing. This type updating frequently stresses the general mission and shape of the church. If pressured, however, all top level renewalists would have to agree that improvement of spirituality and ministry in local settings is a fundamental motive for reforms of any kind, perhaps the key motive. Bishops or bureaucrats would indeed be truant to speak the word "church" apart from people. Simply dressed cardinals still need subjects; mission executives need constituents to receive reports.

Consequently, renewal programs worked up by church leaders always move in implementation from somewhere "out there" to the specific locales. They are non-grass roots although they utilize the language of concrete models, such as those discussed in the preceding chapter. Especially on the Protestant front, this language has been borrowed, even usurped, because it sounds life-giving.

Churches and their units want to "put renewal through," and they are willing to legislate, promulgate or harangue into objective existence the patterns which are arranged. As with

103

Pope Paul, the desire may be for realization of no more than a particular, delimited kind of renewedness. In other cases, the hawking of verbiage may suffice. And for any Christian body, ecumenism—a renewal priority—can be as rigidly programmatic as can opposition to expanded fellowship.

Organizationally sculptured renewal is the most visible type, from the Vatican right down to the small U.S. Church of the Brethren. So many and so similar are approaches, it seems best to spotlight only two, one Protestant and one Catholic. Historically, the Catholic example is oldest, but the United Methodist "New Church for a New World" stands first since it logically follows the closing paragraphs of chapter four.

The amount of criticism of United Methodism punctuating this book may appear unduly heavy. That Church has earlier been cited, so why now focus on its denomination-wide renewal emphasis? What about the Episcopal, Lutheran, Baptist and Presbyterian counterparts? And what about the decade-old Consultation on Church Union? COCU has an enormous, ecumenical case of renewal fever. Early clues on its draft plan of union for uniting the nine member churches point to great stress on parish updating, furnished from the consensus of planners.

Two factors are paramount in opting for the United Methodists. The denomination, with almost 11 million members, is the largest renewal-conscious Protestant Church in the country. Slightly larger, the Southern Baptist Convention finally got around to endorsing racial integration in 1968. This "deliberate" reaction to the 1954 Supreme Court ruling on desegregation suggests why the Southern Baptists are not here treated as solidly in the renewing camp. Along with its size, the United Methodist Church has a clearly delineable structure which facilitates the noting of changes. They may have no theology, but a system the Methodists definitely have.

Second, an appraisal of the United Methodist renewal tack could be synonymous with a look at COCUized American Protestantism of the future. It is well known that if a program requires planning or financing, the Methodists make the best expediters. They have a way with bureaucracy. Methodism is more easily joined than merged with. A COCU Church will be a Methodist Church or the Methodists will not join. Why should they? COCU's other eight members could unite and the United Methodist Church would still be almost as large as the new denomination. These comments are not meant to seem facetious. If or when the institutional churches go down the drain, identifiable Methodists will flow past in organized committees.

The second example of organization-sponsored reform is the predominantly Roman Catholic Liturgical Conference. Rationale for its selection will be recorded later.

The United Methodist "New Church for a New World"

American Methodism has consistently experienced the same cleavage between conservative and liberal wings which marks all major Protestant denominations. In the 20th century, the liberals have gained control of the jargon, but not without concessions to the less open-minded. Sported for decades was a Social Creed blasting racial discrimination. Yet until 1968 a separate, non-geographic jurisdiction for black congregations existed in most of the U.S.

This dichotomy is important in evaluating the renewal face officially put on by the entire church in 1968. Preliminary to that happening must be observations about United Methodist characteristics. The denomination is set on a thoroughly democratic base, at least on paper. It is only quasi-episcopal; bishops, individually or collectively, have no power to make, change or interpret beliefs. They enjoy vast administrative authority in their Areas, usually composed of one or more geographic Conferences. Legislative power is vested in a quadrennial General Conference composed of lay and clerical delegates elected by the conferences.

A supreme court-like Judicial Council can overrule the General Conference on matters involving constitutional interpretation. Five jurisdictions are imposed between the legislating unit and the conferences. Jurisdictional meetings elect bishops. The business of the church at large is run by a bevy of boards, agencies and commissions. All property—frame church buildings in Georgia or major universities—owned by any Methodist group ultimately belongs to the church. No local congregation can break away and keep its property unless it wants to buy it.

Doctrine is loose. Mission work is extensive. Ecumenism is generally not frowned upon. The church is generous in interdenominational works. The U.S. has been good to Methodism, founded in 18th century England by John Wesley. Methodism was good to the young U.S. The frontier history is a classic study in religious and sociological relevance. "Free grace" circuit riders gave the excitement-starved pioneers a gospel of light, love and warmth more vibrant than the dreary Calvinism of the 19th century.

Divisions arose over structure trifles and over slavery. As Methodism became more respectable and stodgy, it spawned the emotion-filled Adventist and Pentecostal groups. The three major Methodist groups got back together in 1939. And then came 1968, when The Methodist Church and the Evangelical United Brethren Church, which shared a German

Wesleyan heritage, merged to form the United Methodist Church.

The Uniting General Conference in Dallas voted an extensive revamp collected together by a Program Council under the heading: "A New Church for a New World." It was a victory for the renewalists at the conference and in the preliminaries. The union gave a fitting occasion for change making. So many new licks were successfully struck at the assemblage that one participant observed that had "the meeting lasted one more day the delegates would have undone everything accomplished because they suddenly were afraid to go home and face the local people." J. Robert Nelson, Boston theologian and head of Methodists for Church Renewal, said: "What the Second Vatican Council has been for the Roman Catholic Church, the Dallas Uniting Conference might be for the United Methodist Church."[1]

Actions of importance included abolition of the all-Negro jurisdiction (automatically phased out in the Plan of Union); virtual termination of a long-standing prohibition on clergy use of alcohol and tobacco; formation of a committee to study the Church's theology; creation of a Commission on Religion and Race to quicken integration and keep an ear tuned to the black community; approval of an investigation of racial and labor charges against the near sacrosanct, multi-million dollar Methodist Publishing House, and passage of a $20 million Fund for Reconciliation, the most ambitious social-economic problems priority ever set by a church.

All this did not happen entirely through Holy Spirit waftings in the Dallas Civic Auditorium. Planning and pressure were involved. Groundwork was laid in revisions of educational materials and methods prior to the merger. Many programs ordered were worked out beforehand by committees. Lobbies proved surprisingly effective.

Black Methodists for Church Renewal was particularly vocal. Under the leadership of James Lawson, a Memphis, Tennessee, pastor and close colleague of the late Martin Luther King, Jr., the black caucus was formed in February 1968. Fully a "church" phenomenon, the black Methodists set out to organize their dissatisfactions with the denomination. High on the list of concerns were "inclusive fellowship at all levels," ending of any structural discrimination, exploration of Methodist union with Negro denominations, support for the discrimination-fighting Project Equality, guarantees of adequate black representation in all agencies and focus on urban areas as the chief mission field of the denomination.

Many of these points were directly won, and the words of the General Conference were supportive of others. Black bishops were subsequently elected to chair important boards. A new Negro bishop was later chosen by an integrated electoral gathering. Another was assigned to an East Tennessee region. Renewal in race relations looked launched. Christianity was endorsed by the Methodists.

A hopefully renewing structure for local congregations was one of the most important ingredients of the Plan of Union. Once passed, it became mandatory for all churches. (Converse to the experience of the United Church of Christ in its union birth several years earlier, the United Methodists lost very few congregations. About fifty former EUB churches in the Pacific Northwest reneged and, abiding by church law, purchased their own property from the denomination.)

The terms for congregational structure were totally revised. Required commissions on education, missions, social concerns, evangelism and stewardship and finance fell before a Council on Ministries, allowing flexibility in setting up working groups and responding to spontaneous task forces. Lay participation was increased. Near-autonomous trustees were placed under the Administrative Board (formerly the Official Board). More decision-making youths were called for. Options were allowed on the extent of local organization, within limits.

The Methodists Needed to Renew

Evidence is available to support a claim that a renewing stab at the local level was scarcely premature. The Earl D. C. Brewer study of 1,318 new Methodist churches, formed between 1950 and 1964, shows high percentages of time and effort spent on self-directed activities. Ranked lowest in a list of fourteen items by lay Official Board chairmen were social action and community-related thrusts which shine brightest on renewal's scoreboard. Three of the top five items pertained to finances. Social concerns itself, distinguished from community projects and interaction, was ranked ninth in time but twelfth in success.[2]

Chairmen of Commissions on Stewardship and Finance found their groups most successful at making written reports of payments to individual members. (They found themselves slightly more adept than interested in stewardship home visitation which utilized a turnover chart.)[3] The most frequent activity of the five required commissions, plus an optional one on worship, was the fact of existence. In no case, except education, did the success of the work come close to approximating the stress on having the commissions. One possible conclusion is that considerable wheelspinning took place.

Another Brewer tabulation points to a need for renewal. Nearly three-fourths of the new congregations were all white, a fourth mostly white and 2.6 per cent all non-white. "Yet they served communities in which only a third of the population was all white but with six out of ten mostly white. Very few new churches had been organized in non-white communities. The all white composition of the church membership did not seem to be related to growth rate or year of organization."[4]

Such a finding gives precise dimensions to the urgency of the Black Methodists for Church Renewal's demands. The Brewer statistics on new churches bear out Earnest A. Smith, a Methodist Social Concerns staff member, speaking at the formation of the black caucus, "Our Church has adopted statements which have never been taken seriously."

On enlivenment of local ministries and in implementation of brotherhood, the Plan of Union and the majority will of the delegates at Dallas were for a season of renewal. A strong "get with it" challenge was issued at the formal merger service by Albert Outler. The Perkins School of Theology professor, no mean critic of foot-dragging in his church, declared: "The church is in radical crisis, and in the throes of a profound demoralization, at every level: of faith and order, life and work. In such times, business as usual simply will not get our business done. Our own past golden age—the heyday of pietism in a pre-urbanized society—has faded. Frontiersmen for tomorrow must be as dynamically adaptive to the new 'new world' as our forefathers were in theirs."[5] Judged by the official record, the challenge was accepted. United Methodists had gone "out there" to Dallas and officially decided to renew. What happened then? Not much besides a great deal of programming, publishing and promoting—"P's" for which Bishop Ralph Ward of Syracuse, New York, has noted "unusual" Methodist skills.[6] Meetings—many local, regional and national—were held with, as the black caucus had asked, a prime stress on urban ministry. *Study Opportunities for Ministers* urged clergy to take part in Summer 1969 renewal seminars, urban training programs and human relations institutes as part of a General Conference directive for updating clergy education. A commission assigned to study and make renewing recommendations on board and agency structure took its caravan to a few grass roots. *The Interpreter*, monthly program magazine, became a picnic of renewal propaganda. Promotion packets proliferated from the high-level offices.

Numerous years will be required before conclusive indications of value from local revamps will be available. The plan could facilitate lethargy as easily as it could revitalize. It could be cumbersome to congregations, such as Germantown Methodist, which were already working toward a style appropriate to situation. It probably will continue to cause confusion, as has happened in church after church finding a shakeup more burdensome busy-work than threat to tradition.

In extolling the greatness of the new system, one pastor told local leaders they could decide to elect eight people to run the whole church, so marvelous was the flexibility. "Well, let's do that and go home," suggested an elderly woman who later asked an associate pastor, "Why does everything the church does have to be so complicated?" She wondered if the members might be more worthy Christians in spending time on community needs instead of overhauling structure patterns. The answer is "no" in a renewal from "out there" approach.

Other spheres of United Methodist renewal took a rest after the General Conference. A special session of the Dallas delegates was scheduled for 1970 to review the progress on merger and reform. Analysts and some bishops asked in 1969 that the meeting be postponed since adequate reflective reports could not be completed. They asked if delegates who approved the special confab could be polled by mail, seeking permission to delay. The Judicial Council ruled negatively. An unnecessary $500,000 meeting stood. Renewing? Such money would buy a chance in life for half a county in Mississippi.

United Methodists, nevertheless, scarcely are alone in letting literal stewardship diverge from established priorities— poverty, race relations, equal employment. Slogans of "crisis in the cities" were at a high point in Summer 1968. The National Council of Churches had its "Crisis" program on paper. Denominations and dioceses were sketching theirs. Funds were an all-important ingredient. Yet the Protestant and Orthodox Churches spent thousands upon thousands to send score upon score of delegates to the World Council's Uppsala, Sweden, Assembly. These churchmen consorted with foreign colleagues about world development, passed resolutions on human problems and gave attention to a theology of renewal. At the last minute, a panel on racism was inserted in the agenda.

The Americans might have stayed home to greater advantage. The money saved could have been spent for some critical need. Perhaps more importantly, renewal and internationalization might vastly have been served by U.S. Churches indicating their trust of overseas brothers. No American churchman proposed saying to the rest of the world, "We have a crisis we must cope with. You conduct the business this year. We trust you."

Domestic urban efforts of denominations also deserve a critical eye when sums of money placed in ghetto banks by churches do not exceed the amount covered by federal depository insurance, and this is the case in more than one instance. Similarly to be questioned are highly publicized "good works," like that of a Lutheran denomination allocating a sizeable sum for urban training with the largest share going to run a coordinator's office. Less than a year after the 1968 Methodist General Conference, more sensitive persons felt required to warn against the huge Fund for Reconciliation being spent on traditional projects.

A negative judgment against a "New Church for a New World" must not, of course, be given prematurely. Pentecosts have been rare for over nineteen centuries. Only a dreamer would hope for overnight modern church relevance. On the other hand, one can legitimately ask if action should not closely follow words in a renewal campaign. A year passed after the April-May 1968 General Conference, and still no report was forthcoming from the committee responsible for investigating the Publishing House. That firm gave serious consideration to membership in Project Equality (joining as supplier rather than contributing sponsor) endorsed by the legislating conference, only after direct and indirect threats of boycott from the black caucus and other Church agencies. The Council of Bishops continued to issue statements linguistically inoffensive, or uninspiring, to Ku Klux Klanners, black militants and anybody in between.

Renewalists entered a period of salesmanship, balancing the spiraling cost of the updating with the joy of relevance. The apostolic era of the book of Acts was seized as model for spirituality and service. Recapture of Pentecost became good subject matter. Said an article in *The Interpreter:* " 'Hold God to his promises,' cried Luther. Pentecost is a good time to hold him to the promise made through Christ to the disciples, 'Lo, I am with you always.' Test him, move out in action and see if his power is not there. Pentecost with all its power may be nearer than you think."[7] But the author of these words was not naive. He continued: "To be honest, Pentecost is not likely to mean much in most churches in 1969. Since they will not move, they cannot receive God's

power and presence. But here and there, pray God, Pentecost
may come to some church. Let loose from there, there is no
telling what may happen to give release to the captive, dignity
to the dehumanized, and hope to men who are in despair."[8]

The assertion is true. But, pray God, does it take an official,
costly renewal program from "out there" to test God and
cause a Pentecost-spreading movement to start in "some
church"?

United Methodist renewal is a word program, adopted and
structured in the absence of anything more creative to do
than perpetuate the organized institution. And holding fast
to the Methodist hand are the other mainline Protestants of
America. The pants-wetting fear which overtook them when
the Black Manifesto asked reparations for complicity in
racism and slavery showed the love for the institutions.

What to Do with Renewal: A Catholic Experience

The Second Vatican Council, along with aftermath implementation, is the most obvious effort to renew a church and
local churches through an overall approach set by top level
decision makers. However, despite the singular importance
of Pope John's calling the Council and despite the official way
in which *aggiornamento* was endorsed, it is wrong to suppose
there were no precursors to Vatican II. Catholics who think
the Council originated ecumenism (and Protestants are sometimes willing to let them think so) live in error. Protestants
who assume nothing with modern edges was honed in Catholicism before the Council are equally misinformed.

Vatican II is also the most significant ecclesiastical updating
enterprise since the 16th Century Reformation, though a
"new Reformation" (with capital "R") it is not. Much has

changed in the church, but the change has been *permitted* by hierarchy in droplets and dribbles rather than in a broad stream. The begrudging paternalism in an officially renewing church is a major reason why *aggiornamento* has turned to revolution on many fronts.

Catholic renewal was the hierarchy's program to begin with. The drives and letups, openness and caginess, promulgations and procrastinations which have paced its course must fit prominently into what Daniel Callahan called "the renewal mess."[9] Those committed to full steam ahead have been forced to play a waiting game; those who wanted to proceed cautiously but steadily have tugged at the same time they have been forced to be defensive, and the conservatives have found their world slipping away. If Catholicism had a deeper, more objective heritage of pluralism, the situation would not be so complex. Never totally monolithic—not even during the most rigid epochs—Catholicism still seems to feel guilty about a rampant lack of unanimity. Post-Vatican II traditionalists, liberals and radicals have, therefore, wanted everybody else, at least in the nation or neighborhood, to sound like themselves.

The developing fate of Vatican Council-type renewal—centralized in an event "out there"—is too complicated to fit into a brief discussion. It must suffice to take a substratum of Catholic reform to illustrate what can happen to a programized approach. Simply put, the following paragraphs are a study in how a renewal "mess" comes about. The example is the National Liturgical Conference of North America. Active participants may be distraught to find themselves classified as a non-grass roots, organization-type renewal pattern. While, prior to 1969, the conference was an association loosely linked to the National conference of Catholic Bishops, it has never stood in main-channel officialdom.

Admittedly, Liturgical Conference renewal does not fit into the same category as the legislated United Methodist "New Church for a New World." Nor is it a small replica of the Vatican Council. The Liturgical Conference is an organization, with a history, which advocated church renewal of particular demeanor and goals. Eclecticism was not its traditional nature, just as Vatican II never conceived of itself as incohesive. In fact, its original motivation was more clearcut than the Council's vague *aggiornamento*. Its story qualifies to mirror the plight of Catholic renewal encouraged in extra-territorial fashion. There is background.

The Liturgical Movement

The liturgical movement in the Roman Catholic Church, including the Eastern Rites, was abetting some Vatican II-type images a half-century before Angelo Giuseppe Roncalli took the papal throne as John XXIII. The Council's *Constitution on the Sacred Liturgy* made authoritative, for example, the democratization of the liturgy called for in 1909 by Dom Lambert Beauduin, O.S.B., at a National Conference of Catholic Action in France. With sanctions from Popes Pius X, Pius XI and Pius XII, national and international liturgical conferences grew.

The early movement did not label itself "renewalist," a term gaining Catholic vogue only in the 1960's. In retrospect, the movement did have an updating aura. It represented renewal from "out there"—at Assisi, Louvain and Lugano (sites of important liturgical meetings), or at the annual national Liturgical Weeks held in the U.S. from 1944, the year in which a permanent Liturgical Conference replaced a Benedictine organization established five years earlier. Goals were not necessarily liberal, but they were definite, double-barrelled aims to emphasize the centrality of liturgy in Christian life and to urge active participation by the laity. Energy was directed both toward the structures of the church, where at times the sponsors felt a lack of appreciation of the liturgical outlook, and to parishes where church members needed instruction in and interpretation of worship.

Pope Pius XII's encyclical *Mediator Dei* in 1947 is considered the charter of the movement, though the pontiff warned against unrest caused in Europe and elsewhere by liturgical concerns, as much as he recognized its importance. Actually, the movement was sometimes drunk on liturgy as the end and be-all of religion, and it could have moved liberally or conservatively depending on the other fellow's treatment of liturgical reality. Especially in relation to emphasis on vernacular worship and extension of liturgical occasions, changes toward the more flexible began to occur. A bilingual ritual for France was approved in 1947; translations into Indian dialects came in 1949; limited evening masses were allowed in Japan and Poland in 1948, and a German edition of the Canon appeared in 1952. Restoration of the Easter Vigil in 1952 complemented the movement's work.

In 1954, English was permitted in portions of the sacraments of baptism, marriage and extreme unction. The U.S. based Liturgical Conference, headquartered in Washington, D.C. was especially concerned with lay involvement in liturgy, though before Vatican II such participation could be little more than reading the rites along with the priest at Mass and making short responses in other services. Again and again the desire for more lay involvement was sounded, but the approach was careful. Renewal of the meaning of the liturgy, a theoretical undertaking, and not reformulation of services was basic. Even in the early 1960's, some active conference members were nervous over potentially "intemperate" no-tions of the Chicago-based Vernacular Society. There was fear that smidgens of novelty might harm chances for approval of vernacular services at the pending Vatican Council.

With the announcement of the Council in 1959, the conference began to prepare itself for the dawning new day. The 1960 Liturgical Week in Pittsburgh had "Liturgy and Unity in Christ" as its theme, and all persons were invited since the subject was of "concern to our separated brethren as well as ourselves." Three hundred Protestant and Orthodox observers were in attendance two years later for a Seattle, Washington, meeting held a few months before Vatican II opened.

This is not to say the Liturgical Conference was prophetic or homogeneously avant-garde. Members had common liturgical goals, but were variously impressed with the rumblings of ecumenism and updating. Revolution or ark rocking was outside the scope, as suggested in the ecumenical observations of a speaker-priest at the 1961 Liturgical Week. He correctly noted the stumbling block set before "ritualistic Protestants" by the Catholic veneration of Mary, and continued:

But they (ritualistic Protestants) are Christians who understand and accept arguments from tradition as well as from Scripture; they earnestly and sincerely desire to identify themselves with pre-tridentine Christianity. If, then, we can show them, by historical research of irreproachably scientific accuracy that the worship of Mary has been an element of all the ancient liturgies, it is hard to see how it could fail to convince them that the worship of Mary is an integral part of traditional Christianity. That would be a great step in the direction of reunion.[10]

An assurance of ecumenical renewal could hardly be more enthusiastically or more Catholicly stated. Perhaps the priest was not completely shattered when ecumenism did not take this particular bent.

The Constitution on the Sacred Liturgy, issued from Vatican II by Pope Paul in December, 1963, both sanctioned and pulled the foundations from under the liturgical movement. Implementation of what had long been proposal was possible, but then the hierarchy, not voluntary Liturgical Conferences, was charged with carrying out liturgical revisions. The liturgical movement was in Limbo during most of Vatican II, even while the Council's Commission on the Liturgy carried out directives of the *Constitution*. Renewal reached local parishes, the speed of introducing more participatory worship being frequently noted. Said one enthusiast: "The Council quickly ceased to be something remote, occupying the bishops gathered at Rome. . . . By sharing actively in worship, even the ordinary Catholic began to take part in the great work launched by Pope John and continued by Pope Paul."[11] (Given this assertion, one does wonder what it means that in *1969* almost half of the constituents of the Diocese of Worchester, Massachusetts, could not meaningfully recognize a reference to the Second Vatican Council!)

The Liturgical Conference assuredly did not complain that renewal was reaching parishes. Vatican II, nevertheless, meant organization reevaluation after the bishops left the final session in late 1965. Important to mention is the seriousness with which much of the liturgical movement took all of the Vatican II documents. The constitution on liturgy was most relevant, yet received as mandate were the letter and spirit of the other constitutions and decrees. The theme of Liturgical Week 1966, the first after the Council, had a fresh, Harvey Cox-influenced thrust, "Worship in the City of Man."

Conversations about liturgical experimentation grew. Prior to the annual August week, two liturgical scholars, Father

Godfrey Diekmann, O.S.B., and Father Eugene A. Walsh, S.S., told a New England Regional Liturgical Conference that experimentation under "controlled circumstance" was necessary if liturgical renewal was to be meaningful. Those in authority, said Father Diekmann, must not become "victims of the previous mentality where everything liturgical had to be legislated." (Honesty requires noting in the case of Father Diekmann that "controlled" was more important than "experimentation" in his proposal.)

The 1966 Liturgical Week program was expanded to reflect Vatican II initiatives. Seminars included "Jesus and Christians in the Modern World," "Singing at Parish Masses," "Liturgical Celebration for Adolescents," "Educating Priests for People's Needs" and "Liturgy and the Intellectual." Non-Catholics were invited as speakers. One of those was Methodist Joseph Mathews of Chicago's Ecumenical Institute who, striking his renewal gong, proclaimed that "God is being born again in our time."

Buds of social action bloomed at the 1966 meeting. Speaking on "A World Come of Age in Christ," Sister M. Charles Borromeo declared that "we Catholics stand shamed at our utter lack of awareness or responsibility before the structured evils of racism, discrimination, urban decay, a sensational press, the horror of war and nuclear armament." In true Liturgical Conference heritage, social action was linked to the local parish, with Father John E. McCarthy of Houston advocating appointment of directors in all inner-city parishes to spearhead activities based on Catholic social doctrine.

Liturgical Week, 1967, in Kansas City—in which 10,000 were involved—wrenched open the period of renewal "mess" into which the conference moved. Since then, the movement has been as passionate, as halting, as shoulder-peeking and as rifted as the general Catholic fabric. Faced is a question standing square before mild, moderate or roaring renewalist: "In God's name, what do we do now?" What happened?

Gaping differences in opinions arose. Participants who believed Vatican II had taken care of liturgical renewal felt inclined to disband. Msgr. John J. McEneany, conference president, responded to this group by deploring complacency toward further renewal. He stood with those Richard John Neuhaus, the Lutheran man-about-liturgy, later described as "painfully aware of the gap between conciliar statement and parochial reality."[12] On the other hand, Msgr. McEneany stood against the liturgically tired who suggested that "this conference take up other causes." Against these, he defended the emphasis on liturgy.

Two factors combined to give a social action and not-so-controlled hue to the Week. First was an article by Daniel Callahan in the *National Catholic Reporter* a few days prior. He proposed "Putting Liturgy in Its Place." A substitute for "devaluated" liturgy is social action. Model for a shift was at hand. In Kansas City the Liturgical Week trailed the annual meeting of the National Catholic Conference for Interracial Justice, attended by a large delegation of blacks who put "soul" into the worship arranged around the civil rights sessions. Numerous persons were present for both meetings.

The Liturgical Conference went much farther in Kansas City than it had ever gone before in worship experimentation. Nothing much happened at the much touted opening "happening," but a socially activating, ecumenically invigorating and liturgically pioneering direction was taken. The conference bypassed a role as mere servant to the reforms of the Council. The phrase "loyal opposition" to the bishops was heard. The coherence between theoretical and practicing liturgist began to split.

A thirty-six-member board of directors took up the cause of defending renewal against growing retrenchment of the hierarchy and the course of extending renewal beyond permission-gathering for desired innovations. In October, 1967, the board rather timidly announced support for extra-territorial parishes and home masses. "We would not pretend to guess at future developments, but we plead for openness and we have nothing but praise for the dioceses where these developments have been encouraged, where the Spirit has been allowed to blow where He wills."

Three months later the board untimidly charged the U.S. hierarchy with failure to provide "open, creative, and vigorous leadership" in the liturgical movement. Prediction was made that disregard for the bishops' liturgical authority would "become even more widespread if the quality of episcopal leadership is not upgraded."

All was not well within the board, but the tension did not come to the fore until immediately after the 1968 Liturgical Week, held in Washington, D.C. The theme, "Revolution: Christian Response," was viciously attacked by the *Catholic Standard,* Washington archdiocesan newspaper, before the conference met. Further, no diocesan sponsorship was sought for the Week, as had been the case for twenty-seven previous years. Patrick Cardinal O'Boyle dissociated his princedom from the meeting and, in effect, condemned it. Plans continued, and the event was held with some 4,500 participants.

The sessions ended with resolutions far afield from the once-upon-a-time appeals for lay participation in worship. Black power—defined as the "right of black people . . . to control their communities"—was endorsed along with the churches' right to use economic power for social action and justice under the law. Continuing parish renewal incentives, the conference asked churches to "demand that local courts and police execute justice rather than mere control." Compared to the statement marking backgrounds of certain Protestant judicatories or the National Council of Churches, there was nothing startling in the actions. What was new was these particular issues taking the foreground during Liturgical Week.

In the eyes of Cardinal O'Boyle and some Conference leaders, the organization had begun to flirt with revolution rather than respond to it. Dissatisfied board members were essentially those who in 1967 opted for retention of the liturgy focus. Partly because unleavened bread was used in a Jazz Mass closing the week, five directors resigned. "Irresponsible administrations . . . and mismanagement" was suggested. Included were Msgr. McEneany and Bishop Charles A. Buswell of Pueblo, Colorado, one of the two bishops on the board. Supposedly, promises to Cardinal O'Boyle had been broken, leading one resignee to score "disregard of universal and local Church law," which results in increased difficulty for officials taking the Liturgical Conference seriously.

John Mannion, former executive secretary of the conference who left the staff before the 1968 Liturgical Week, subsequently noted that the persistent complaint of critics and even some well-disposed persons was, "What does all this have to do with liturgy?"[13]—a reference to civil rights figures, political scientists, urban organizers and a Communist strategist on the program. Said Mannion: "Granted that the subjects of this meeting are the subjects that should occupy all men, is it the Liturgical Conference's mission to pursue them or not? Can the Conference handle these larger issues and also sustain its work in specifically liturgical matters?. . . .

What the 1968 Week revealed is that the program planners
are substantially ahead of their clientele—by and large a
good thing."[14]

Good thing or bad, it was the course of "devaluated"
liturgy which was pursued, with hope as a revolutionary
motif planned as the 1969 Liturgical Week theme. A preliminary discussion called hope "the stuff of revolution, the
seed of progress. So hope is a point where Christian meets
with every man who has not surrendered to despair and to
futility. The sacred-secular 'dichotomy' is here explored, if
not resolved. Secular humanists here confront Christian
humanists, asking searching questions . . . and being asked."[15]
(The theme finally selected for 1969 was "Celebration of
Man's Hope." The agenda suggested that the liturgical and
the social was at the forefront of Liturgical Conference
thinking. It looked strangely like what might be left over
should the Living Theater perform "The Cocktail Party.")

Such language is really not boldface radicalism. Actually,
it sounds lifted out of the 1966 World Council of Churches'
World Conference on Church and Society. Yet it is a long,
long way from "Singing at Parish Masses." The renewalist
is still talking about revolution, not practicing it.

Predictably, the board of directors announced in early
1969 an inclusive ecumenical policy (Protestant board members and a Protestant staffer were added in 1968) and re-
defined itself as "a voluntary association with no formal,
exclusive, institutional ties." Liturgical renewal can assuredly transcend sectarianism, but the abandonment of formal
Catholic ties—if the Conference is serious—does raise an
interesting question about its fostering of parish councils.
Lay councils were sanctioned in Vatican II's *Decree on the
Apostolate of the Laity.* Development of such units has been
a priority of the Liturgical Conference. A monthly publica-

tion called *Parish Council* emerged in 1968, containing "here's how" as well as general information on parish council edification. In this concern, close ties were made with associations of laymen. *Parish Council* also spreads the word on experimental worshipping communities, such as Nova (New) in the Diocese of Richmond. (Nova is a group of families and some priests who "asked to celebrate Mass together each Sunday, while at the same time studying ways the liturgy and their lives could be more fully directed to the worship of God and to Christ's service in the world.")[16]

The policy on ecumenism stated that publications would be oriented toward the needs of Catholic and other Christian communities. The issue of *Parish Council,* following the policy, contained not a single non-Catholic entry. It must be doubted whether the Liturgical Conference can continue specific Catholic programs in an ecumenical framework. Protestants have enough to worry about without getting into hot water with Catholic bishops over parish councils! But to give up the Catholic thrust for ad hoc ecumenism means the Conference loses its reason for being. Another helping-hand ecumenical agency, yea a voluntary one, is at best a non-contribution to the ecclesiastical haystack.

Renewalist to the hilt in language, given a tinge of revolution occasionally, the Liturgical Conference has nothing to renew. Official Catholicism has its own program. Lacking strategically placed episcopal support and opting out of the institutional Catholic fold, it has no direct route to parishes except through priest and lay members and in newsletters to parish councils. There is also a homily service, a subscription program whereby priests are provided suitably renewing sermons. The idea has merit in the context of organization-proposed *aggiornamento* and in light of the relative inability of clergymen of any variety to prepare bearable, intelligent sermons. Essentially, however, any merchandising of standardized homilies—for Protestant or Catholic consumption —is a gimmick and a sop. If a sermon is required in a worship service, any clergyman who cannot prepare appropriate comments for a congregation among whom he lives had best turn in the collar. Pipelined inspiration is poor substitute for renewal. St. Paul had some words about "clanging cymbals," a good description for any sermon service.

The Liturgical Conference is probably not basically responsible for the "mess" it got into. It did not tend toward embryonic revolutionary language until doors began to be slammed in its face. It probably took Vatican II too seriously, given a hierarchy committed to only a little fresh air through slightly opened windows. On the other hand, it probably took itself too seriously, wanting all to elect its path. Religion— even the liberal sort—is frightfully intolerant.

Vatican II swept up the liturgical movement. The brand of life the Liturgical Conference sought in perpetuating itself and in serving the church was not welcomed by American Catholicism. Strangely, renewal became a threat to renewal, indicating that the officially sponsored *aggiornamento* is the only type the institutional church wants. Church renewal, it seems, does not welcome challenges from church renewal.

A movement which loses its history, as the Liturgical Conference did, and has its future blocked can do almost nothing. Can it even maintain a viable identity? Reform is not reform on its own confession. Renewal or reform are designations to be given in retrospect. The Liturgical Conference has the alternatives of being outside pressure groups, a church of its own, or a yazoo-type stream never reaching a place to pierce the separating wall. If it finds a future, it will get a name.

Meanwhile, the controllers of Roman Catholicism do not want renewal to rack up too much change. Renewal, please, but only enough *aggiornamento* to keep the wheels of Mother Church clipping round and round. Denizens of the 21st century own the right to decide if Vatican II, or any other renewal effort, was renewing. Prediction of a question in 2039: There was a Church Council in Rome in the 1960's. What was it called? Was it "Lateran"?

Notes

[1] "The Week in Religion," Religious News Service (May 18, 1968).

[2] *A Study of New Church Development, 1967,* carried out by Earl D. C. Brewer, with the assistance of Marie Townsend, through the Religious Research Center, Candler School of Theology, Emory University, Atlanta, Georgia. Sponsored by the Department of New Church Development, Section of Church Extension, the National Division of the Methodist Board of Missions, p. 21.

[3] *Ibid.,* p. 23.

[4] *Ibid.,* p. 63.

[5] Text distributed by United Methodist Information.

[6] In an address to the United Methodist Program Council, St. Louis, Mo. (February 25, 1969).

[7] Carl E. Keightley, "How Far to Pentecost?" *The Interpreter* (April 1969), p. 12. Reprinted with permission.

[8] *Ibid.*

[9] Daniel Callahan, "The Renewal Mess," *Commonweal* (March 3, 1967).

[10] Father Julian Stead, S.S.B., cited in "The Week in Religion," Religious News Service (August 18, 1962).

[11] C. J. McNaspy, S.J., Introduction to *The Constitution on the Sacred Liturgy, The Documents of Vatican II,* ed. Walter M. Abbott, S.J. (New York: The America Press, 1966), p. 135.

[12] Richard John Neuhaus, "The Bishop's Loyal Opposition," *Commonweal* (September 22, 1965), pp. 565-566.

¹³ John Mannion, "Liturgical Week: Too Far Ahead of the Crowd?" *Commonweal* (September 20, 1968), p. 614.

¹⁴ *Ibid.*, pp. 614-615.

¹⁵ "Is Christianity Hopeless?" *Liturgy* (October, 1968).

¹⁶ Dolores R. Leckey, "The Nova Community," *Parish Council* (March 1969), p. 3.

6 / Renewal City U.S.A.

Come from the four winds, O breath, and breathe
upon these slain, that they may live (Ezek. 37:9).

Chicago has many descriptive labels competing with "Windy City." None is more fitting, or as surprising in terms of the city's less than sterling political reputation, than "laboratory of church renewal." Chicago contains more renewal groups and centers than any place in the world. Most represent an institute-type renewal, a missional approach to parish restructure, urban problems, ecumenical ministry and community involvement. The type differs from congregational models, denominational programs or amorphous organizations. The institutes and centers of Renewal City, U.S.A., are specific, concrete and instructional.

Added to the institutes is an extensive theological community of nineteen seminaries or graduate schools of theology with a combined enrollment over 2,800. And part of the Protestant and Catholic establishment share suburban Evanston with the Baha'i Faith and the Loop with the Wrigley Building. Name a church thing; Chicago's got it.

The city makes a good case for itself as church renewal laboratory setting. It is known as a "typical" (remember the 1968 Democratic Convention?) American metropolis in contrast, notably, to New York, which is atypical. Large Protestant and Catholic communities, with traditionally strong structures, abide on Lake Michigan's southern shore. It has chic, culture and ghettos; future-forming universities and political ward bosses; the supposedly stabilized Mid-Westerner and the rural emigrant. The Church Federation of Greater Chicago *was,* for a half-decade, one of the most adventurous church associations in the nation, pioneering and ready to risk. (The federation either risked or slipped, for its health seems to be poor.)

Chicago is mainstream, unlike New York where everybody is a member of an ethnic group or moved there because, at least to a Pakistani official at the United Nations, "it is the capital of the world." But Chicago is the religious capital of the U.S., and there experiments and innovations can gain disciples. The best way to show the nature and types of institute renewal in Chicago is to list and discuss some of the laboratories. Congregation/geographic models, of course, are included in the city's makeup, and denominational patterns are not outlawed. Yet very little falling under a renewal rubric in Chicago could stand in isolation from the experimenting institutes.

Laboratory A: The Ecumenical Institute

The Ecumenical Institute (EI) has attracted the greatest attention and spread its wings farther than any renewal operation other than Vatican II. It began when a group from the Faith and Life Community in Austin, Texas—the organization earlier mentioned as having helped students in religious foundations at the University of Texas get "with it"—accepted the offer of the Church Federation to come to Chicago and found an ecumenical experiment. Impetus for the institute followed the 1954 Evanston Assembly of the World Council of Churches. Headed by the charismatic Joseph Mathews, a Methodist and brother of the bishop of Boston, a beachhead was established in 1962 on the West Side in the facilities of a former Church of the Brethren seminary. EI began its move "into all the world."

An impartial observer or critiquer of EI is practically nonexistent. It arouses strong support or strong opposition. Middle ground about EI is narrow. The purpose is defined as "research and training center dedicated to the task of the renewal of the church through the renewal of the local congregation, for the sake of the entire world." Goals are verbally that simple and that inclusive!

The work is divided into three sections: (1) national and international teaching programs, (2) the Fifth City community reformulation project, and (3) the resident faculty community. Headquarters are in Chicago, but instruction is global. The curious and the converted not only come from all parts of the world to the homebase, EI goes to them through twenty-four centers—Canada, England, Australia, Japan and India. To hear of an EI outpost in China or the Soviet Union would hold little surprise.

Fifth City is a sixteen-block ghetto neighborhood surrounding the institute. Everybody who lives in that prescribed territory is a part of Fifth City, whether they know or like the idea. It is like being born into the Church of Sweden or into an Episcopal family in Tidewater, Virginia. Existence equals membership. In EI understanding, responsibility to the community means staying with the community, a step beyond the "colonizing" mentality of some urban programs. The institute has explained: "The intention of the 5th City project in community reformulation is the development of a practical operating model as a demonstration of what serious, responsible and significant mission for the local congregation could be."[1] In developing community, EI says it points toward the church working itself out of a job.

A number of educational, fellowship, rehabilitation and

citizenship opportunities are offered in Fifth City. The success is not easily measured. Indigenous officers are elected from the community, but control has tended to remain centralized in the institute. Stephen Rose, for one, has criticized the Fifth City plan as another of the "well-meaning white programs for black people . . . seen by some blacks as an impediment to the necessary task of turning the ghetto over to the indigenous community."[2] Some truth lurks in the observation, particularly since Rose preceded it by noting that on the night Martin Luther King, Jr. was killed (April 4, 1968), residents of Fifth City set EI afire.

The residential commune of some 200 interns, fellows and permanent participants is at the heart of the Institute. Worship, for which they arise at 6:15 a.m., is the center of the experience, with study and discipline the complements. Scores of hundreds have spent intensive weekends in a course called Religious Studies I, the basic curriculum offering, during which instruction is given in "The Theological Revolution of the 20th Century." But in 1968 there were sixteen other courses in religious and cultural studies.

In terms of the waves of enthusiasm which genuinely emanated from EI, its renewal approach can claim a kind of success. The conservative *Christianity Today* has admitted that "something noteworthy is happening," although EI "is not a community under the Word. What it espouses is a kind of secular humanism. . . ."[3] Appeal has touched Protestants, Catholics and some Jews. Reasons for the EI boom include Mathews, who stimulates excitement and loyalty among his supporters. EIers become missionaries for the renewal type and preach and pass the word (small "w"). The missional outlook is, however, probably the base. EI is unscathingly positive about the possibility of renewing the church and the world through the local congregation.

Congregations are viewed as *the* center of *the* task, world renewal. To the local church and the local pastor bogged down by pessimism at home and the regional and national prophets of gloom, EI comes to say, "we take you seriously." It is no mystery why parish clergymen have latched on to EI. The institute is also able to instill a new fervor for worship in clergymen or laymen coming under the influence. Nor is this surprising, given the stress on worship in Christianity and the fact that worship has lost its appeal in recent years. A boost for this traditional apparatus is taken as God-sent.

EI talks about worship in terms of the "rhythm" of the community's life. Clergy-laity distinctions are broken down. Mechanicalism is scorned—physical exertion included. EI operates like a church, terming itself the embodiment of a "corporate mind." It dreams and practices democratic cohesion, offering itself as a model for the cosmos.

Yet all the scorecards do not let EI win the renewal contest. The fundamentalist Protestant or Catholic naturally rejects it, but he is not really in the renewal picture. Strong opposition is raised by church bureaucrats and by the more radically minded. Church executives who have a denominational program of their own might simply find EI a threat. The same goes for Protestant bishops who have literally put EI devotees out of their parishes. More than challenges to authority may be included in EI opposition. It is arrogant and dogmatic: Mathews has claimed, for example, that the essential theological task of the church is done. Such a statement implies communal—not ecclesiastical—triumphalism; EI is imperialistic.

Strong criticism is often voiced by supporters. John Vincent, the closely heard English Methodist, has said: "After all the criticism has been made you are still stuck with the fact that the Ecumenical Institute has done something."[4]

EI's reception in many parts of the world testifies to what Stephen Rose calls "the parched wasteland of Protestant renewal." (Catholicism can be added.)

Appreciative criticism does not remove the suspicion that EI may not be what it claims to be, that is, a tool for renewal of congregations. Militant converts are leading it increasingly toward a para-church, which does not renew the existing church but results in a new structure and sect. Rose states, "When EI comes more and more into contact and conflict with established institutions in the church, we shall see whether it capitulates to obscurantism and sectarianism, or whether it is made of sterner stuff."[5]

Once, EI said of the Chicago community that "all those who are part of it understand that the time will come when it will have to be replaced or destroyed."[6] Much weeping and gnashing of teeth among the faithful would follow such action. Para-church marks become ever more indelible. The EI order, discipline, worship and outreach is carried afar to its own cadres (embryonic churches?). The EI courses are taught by EI indoctrinated who do not modify or rearrange (dogma?). Neither apostates nor the unbaptized can teach (magisterium?). No criticism is heard except from the inside (officialdom?). Some EI based cadres have moved beyond the model, not always to institute rejoicing (schismatics?).

Few of the leaders have had regular contact with local congregations for years. The Fifth City project has made little overture to the community churches, perhaps grounds for accusing it of paternalism toward the ghetto. EI's fate is not linked to local churches, though the fate of congregations could be linked to EI. The institute is there, growing. Its corporation observes: "That seven families could develop a national educational program that literally spans the nation and the world out of literally nothing is an absurdity, yet it has happened."[7] In EI eyes, the power of the absurd is the will of God. Whether the institute will let that same absurdity put it out of business when enough ambassadors have been sent into the church and world to accomplish renewal remains to be tested. Mothers have been known to strangle their children. Institutes, like institutions, find thoughts of death unpleasant.

Laboratory A: A Renewal Caucus

A renewal caucus exists in the Northern Illinois Conference (Chicago) of the United Methodist Church, composed chiefly of young clergymen who have completed the initial course —some more—at the Ecumenical Institute.[1] Members have moved a judicatory above the congregation in renewal efforts. Their goal is the updating of the geographic conference, a level of Methodism still under renewal-possibility study in the denomination. The United Methodist annual conference is the most clearly political entity in the vast organization. The Northern Illinois renewal caucus reflects a kind of "new politics" in action within the church.

Lobbies have long dotted the ecclesiastical meeting map, usually as ad hoc groups developing in support, or opposition to one-shot agenda items. Or they have been secretive power brokers behind the scenes. The Chicago caucus is highly visible, strategy conscious and long-range in intentions. What distinguishes it from the national black caucuses in denominations is merely whiteness. Most members are white, men who are sensitive to the urban crisis and who are concerned that the church is insensitive.

Aims are openly political, one key target of revision being the appointive system for clergy, a phenomenon peculiar (in Protestantism) to Methodism. Bishops assign ministers in consultation with a cabinet of district superintendents. Age, last salary and pals are some of the criteria for appointment-making. The caucus insisted, prior to appointment-making time in the Summer, 1969, that clergy assignment take account of a man's ability. A strike was even threatened, an interesting novelty, but highly risky for nonessential professionals in a secular world.

In the Chicago setting, the emergence of the renewal caucus in the Methodist Conference illustrates preoccupation with renewal—Methodists have flocked to EI—as well as a projection of change-making beyond the congregation. This could indicate a falling away from renewal stress among young clergy in congregations. Was enthusiasm stymied in communities redirected to institutional targets? Possibly, but probably not. While the caucus has "asked for," it actually seems to want to "get away from," escape the heavy hand of bureaucracy. "Give us ministries we can relate to and leave us alone," the group said in effect. Technically, this is more church decentralization than church renewal broadly defined. Methodists would be well served to study their Presbyterian colleagues who are free to find a situation in keeping with their vision of ability. The Presbyterian clergy is no less troubled than the Methodists, albeit without bishops.

The danger of a renewal crusade against church institutions lies in letting genuine ministerial energy be co-opted by the institutions' wills and won'ts. Victory brings depression because the motive is gone.

Laboratory B: The Urban Training Center

Begun in 1964, the Chicago Urban Training Center (UTC) devotes its program to bringing forth ministries developing "Reflected action at many new points of decision and move-

ment in metropolis." UTC reflective action is to be "rooted
in the understanding and imperatives of one's faith." Initially formed and funded ecumenically, the center quickly
established relations with other communities, including
academia. It approaches the religious and social scene with
substantial seriousness. Private foundations as well as denominational grants support the effort.

UTC gets about 300 students per year for in-service
training, plus others through its special relationship with
the Divinity School of the University of Chicago and the
Chicago Theological Seminary. Long- and short-term experiences are offered. The short usually involves four weeks
in residence, three weeks back home and another month at
the center. The plan is introduction, transposition and reflection. Long-term may range from three months to two years,
in which a student is given the chance to specialize in some
specific aspect of urban life and ministry.

UTC trains to "send forth," as does EI, but minus a
"corporate mind" about rhythmic moods in mission. It is a
school for renewal rather than incipient church. No plans for
infiltrating the church's institutions with stereotyped agents
are laid. Risk centers in people who hopefully have a faith.

An initial part of the training is the "plunge." Students
are sent into the slums of Mayor Richard Daley's domain for
several days with nothing but the clothes on their backs and
a small sum of money. Subsequent reports often recount
revelations—even recognition of acts of kindness among
derelicts.

A strategizing sociological and theological approach is
carried into the situations and decisions trainees face. This
applies also to seminarians from UTC-affiliated schools. The
four-year Doctor of Ministry program at the University of
Chicago's divinity school includes a six-month period within

and under the center. Students are provided urban assign-
ments to work in and bring into UTC training.

Biblical heritage and worship play significant roles in the
reflective side of the program. The center is perhaps a laboratory for relativizing theological education rather than an
example of a church renewal enterprise. For the seminarian
or the active pastor who enrolls, the expanding of educational
experience and the deepening of sensitivity are foremost. A
locally oriented Chicago Action Training Program at UTC
is scoped to serve black clergymen and probe white racism.

UTC's curriculum deals informally with the church as
such. A 1968 course list included nothing more ecclesiastically labeled than an offering on the black church as a model
of power and as a new institution. For the most part, the
structures of religion as they exist are accepted in outline.
The church's responses to racism, black power, economics and
politics get the attention.

Since the center does not pretend to be a model for church
renewal but an agent for the renewal the churches have said
they want, its future should be followed closely. If it is too
late for the church to learn—as some suggest—UTC could
easily benefit the secular men who would find the ways to
make cities of men liveable.

Laboratory C: The Community Renewal Society

Formerly the Chicago City Missionary Society, the Community Renewal Society (CRS) is headed by Donald Benedict,
one of the founders of the East Harlem Protestant Parish.
CRS has an urban thrust and serves as the mission arm of the
United Church of Christ in Chicago. The calling of the organization, Benedict says, "is to renew the metropolis through

faith in action," a modern phrase in mainstream renewalism.

To attain the goal, the society has developed a wide range of programs. One was the crusading *Renewal* magazine, which in the late 1960's is in considerable need of new life itself. Major continuing projects are Toward Responsible Freedom and a Model Cities Technical Assistance Program, both requiring multi-million dollar funding. At the same time, CRS remains involved in traditional inner-city church and settlement house work. It has taken the black-white schism seriously and stirred about to bridge it.

The society is strikingly renewalist out of the classic era of the early 1960's. Revolution has not crept in, or perhaps the revolutionists have crept out. In mid-1969 an executive, speaking to a group of church leaders, lamented the failure of the United Church of Christ to start new congregations in the preceding five years, an undertaking de-emphasized by most urban experts. There was also a plea for church relevance and an urging for funds. CRS takes its place alongside the church institutions. It has a program to sell.

Laboratory D: The North Side Cooperative Ministry

The North Side Cooperative Ministry (NSCM) is not unique in its interreligious composition or community concerns, though it was given an unusual vehicle through which to come to national attention: the 1968 Democratic Convention. As the police prepared for the coming of youthful protesters, so did the North Side clergy. In pairs, several scores (including some nuns) walked the streets and sauntered around Lincoln Park, the site of most of the confrontations between demonstrators and officers of the law. They urged calm, as clergy are expected to do in such situations.

And they did more—treating the wounded, getting the endangered into the shadows and staying with it day and night.

NSCM incorporates clergy from twenty-three churches in an area of 320,000 people, an economically and racially mixed section of opulence and abject poverty. Cooperative as opposed to organic, there is a covenant relationship and a staff coordinator. An unprojective unit, the ministry group is a laboratory of the oldest Christian kind—it served when it was needed. It will again.

Chicago Potpourri

The Ecumenical Institute, Union Training Center, Renewal Society and North Side Ministry are abetted in renewing Chicago Christianity by other groups, such as the Baptist Renewal Society, Chicago Conference on Religion and Race and local church work like that of the First Presbyterian Church, Woodlawn, among South Side street gangs. It all adds up to quite a collection. Renewal is the key word for the church in Chicago, Protestantism anyway. Catholics are participants in all the laboratories mentioned, but the Archdiocese itself still retains leadership of a mostly conservative type.

Where has it led? God alone knows the answer. Project Equality, the anti-discrimination in employment organization, found inroad-making virtually impossible, though the headquarters of the National Catholic Conference for Interracial Justice, the project originator, is in Chicago.

Renewal in Chicago basically takes the institutional church as it is. Pushing and shoving occurs against open recalcitrance. Social action talk is pivotal. Little attention has been given to the foundations of the church. As institutions, the church is based on structures rather than gospel. Renewal of structures requires appraisal of them. But renewal in Chicago has not gone into a far country in exile from the institutions. The energy seems encased. With all its institutes and centers, Chicago is no more renewed than any other American city.

Perhaps the Chicago scene points to why the church is in the mangled shape it is today—no one has done the necessary homework on what a viable church institution might be like. Church and society conferences characteristically end up as "society conferences." A contemporary impasse might have been avoided had a new climate for exploration—something like the Urban Training Center—been set up twenty years ago, a place for theology and sociology to talk together, yell at each other if necessary. Psychology had to first have its day as theology's mate, and whoever thought anything could be learned about church or society by exclusively studying paranoids was mistaken.

Notes

[1] *Image,* the journal of the Ecumenical Institute (Summer 1967), p. 7.

[2] Stephen C. Rose, "The Ecumenical Institute: Ode to a Dying Church," *Christianity and Crisis* (November 11, 1968), p. 268.

[3] *Christianity Today,* Editorial, (April 26, 1968), p. 28.

[4] Interview on April 12, 1969, New York City.

[5] Rose, *op. cit.,* p. 270.

[6] *Image, op. cit.,* p. 270.

[7] *Manpower for Mission,* New Forms of the Church in Chicago, Henry Clark, ed. (New York: Council Press, 1968), p. 33.

7 / Black Man—White Church

And as I looked, there were sinews on them, and
flesh had come upon them, and skin had covered
them; but. . . . (Ezek. 37:8).

If church renewal in general is in a pallid state, renewal puts black churchmen in an even more precarious situation.

The next few years will be crucial for the future of the church. Even more important for some of us, the next few years will determine whether the predominantly white Christian church can receive the "new wine" black Christians have to share. If it shows that it cannot, then, we must modestly say, it has lost the chance of a lifetime. And some of us will begin to create the necessary new wineskins.[1]

So writes a black member of a white church, and he puts the delicate nature of his circumstance and his ultimatum in perspective. There is now no turning back from the issue. The black community is going to move. Movement with it by the white church is up to the whites.

Black American Christians have a two-pronged renewal dilemma: to recall to a white-dominated nation the freedom for all colors promised by citizenship and to assert blackness as part of a whitewashed religion. Whether nation or church can be blackened to an appropriate degree remains to be seen. Renewal inadequate to the black man's needs and

142

rights is no church renewal at all. If the new breed of articulate, demanding and still hopeful black churchmen turns
thumbs down on received denominations or ecumenism for
perpetuating discriminatory or paternalistic religious styles,
the history of the church and its renewal is over.

Renewal Began on Black Turf

Recent church renewal began on black turf. The inner city
ghetto was the first territory, and the white church did not fare
well. As urban whites beat their hasty retreat to the suburbs, a
familiar pattern developed for formerly proud city churches:
rapidly declining memberships, various attempts at consoli-
dation and team ministry, sale of the property and then trans-
fer out from the center of the metropolis. People in cities
were not lacking. Plenty of people remained. They just
were not the church's kind of people. Some sect-type churches,
often storefront, developed and prospered.

Mainline Protestantism made stabs. Considerable resources
were directed to the inner city, and some of the most able
clergy gave themselves to the cause. The East Harlem
Protestant Parish was the most notable (and romantic!) of
these efforts. Many of its leaders—for example, William
Stringfellow, George Webber and Donald Benedict—were
the avant-garde of the 1950's and the early 1960's. (A fuller
account of the Parish is given in chapter four.) And these
white, liberal efforts did contribute for a time to the ghetto
struggles. "Clergy found more to do outside in the streets
and meeting halls of the community than behind the stained
glass windows. . . . As involvement grew, for all intents and
purposes the mission of the church became one with the
black struggle for justice."[2] However, this was only in the

ghetto. The church at large remained aloof, and during this same time the black revolution was brewing and black leadership was growing.

With the black revolution came an end to most inner city white-dominated ministries. "The entire missions structure of mainline Protestantism has had to shift major gears. While a few short years ago the problem was finding the time to do all that was called for, today more and more time is spent trying to find what to do."[3]

Much of the white effort that previously went into the inner city is being redirected to the overcoming of white racism. Malcolm Boyd recalls Stokely Carmichael telling him to get out to suburbia if he wanted to do anything for blacks. The journalistic popularizing of white racism's hold on the nation, following the release of the Kerner Commission report in 1968, gave the church an ideological replacement for white ghetto involvement. The assumption is being made by whites that renewal's racial implications can be handled— justice and participation bestowed—by dealing with white racism. Only good could result from the self-considered or nominal Christian giving up prejudices. The renewal-minded church white, however, has nothing to be arrogant about in attacking a national disease. Its jargon and its practice have too often diverged.

The role of the church in causing or destroying white racism was missing in the Kerner Commission study. According to one story—too good to be apocryphal—a priest asked a commissioner about the omission. "Oh, is the church supposed to be important in this kind of work?" came the reply. The quip is superficial but jolting. As black novelist James Baldwin has said, "We won our Christianity, our faith . . . not because of the example afforded by white Christians, but in spite of it." It was racism that called most of the separate black churches into existence; it is white racism that is calling the black man out of the white churches. Racism is an affront to the gospel, and because the white church has not cleaned its house, the black man has historical evidence to support him when he says, ". . . the fact that, beyond an altogether meaningless tokenism, white Protestantism is either incapable of ridding itself of a pernicious racist ideology and practice or unwilling to do so."[4] And a Roman Catholic voice adds, "The Roman Catholic Church is a racist institution."[5] To talk of structures, new life, revival and new theologies is to use platitudes of the first magnitude until the white church rids itself of racism. Questions of structure and theology which naturally raise themselves must follow rather than precede this problem.

The test of church as renewal agent is to face this issue with all it implies; otherwise, it *must* give away all claims to being a reforming body. To tackle racism will mean controversy, schism and unpopularity. It will mean a loss of members, money and ministers. It may mean a recovery of mission and identity for the remnant remaining.

Black Strategies

Several strategies for fighting racism have been taken by black Christians in the life of the white churches.* (Renewal

* The Black Manifesto, issued on April 26 by the National Black Economic Development Conference (NBEDC), contained a definite strategy for fighting racism, namely, demands to the white religious institutions for $500 million (later $3 billion) in reparations for black development projects. Though the Manifesto's chief champion, James Forman, is not technically a "churchman," the principle of reparations and the Manifesto itself gained wide approval among black leaders within white Churches, Catholic and Protestant. The National Com-

within the black churches is a different problem entirely.)
One proposal, of course, is separatism—"come apart now and
perhaps when we have solved our own problems we can return." This approach has lacked immediate appeal to black
churchmen, probably because of a lingering theological hope
for unity. Charles Spivey, director for social justice of the
National Council of Churches, and a black man, feels that
"black churchmen will stay in the white church and fight
for change—until such time as it becomes obvious that the
white church cannot or will not exorcise white racism. If
this proves to be the case, blacks will have to withdraw."[6]

The most tried recourse has been the caucus, and black
caucuses have appeared in almost every major white Christian
church in the United States, usually made up almost totally
of clergy. These groups have found a kind of umbrella in
the National Committee of Black Churchmen. It was origi-
nally "Negro Churchmen" but, by its second national gathering in October, 1968, had changed to Black. Into this
conference have been drawn nearly all the major black Protestant units, certainly all the caucuses operating in the white
denominations.

Counterparts to black Protestant caucuses exist in Ameri-

---

mittee of Black Churchmen was particularly insistent that Churches
respond positively to NBEDC demands to be recognized as representative of black interests. Manifesto developments brought black threats
of withdrawal from white denominations unless affirmative action was
forthcoming. Greater recognition of black leadership in the church
was an inevitable result of the prolonged controversy caused by the
document. The Manifesto phenomenon intensified, rather than altered,
the discussion of black church renewal found in this chapter. For a
thorough study of the challenge to white church institutions and impact
upon black churchmen, see *Black Manifesto: Religion, Racism and
Reparations*, edited and introduced by Robert S. Lecky and H. Elliott
Wright (New York: Sheed and Ward, 1969).

can Catholicism on national and diocesan levels. A black priest group, the Black Clergy Caucus, developed in 1968 during the National Clergy Conference on the Interracial Apostolate in Detroit. The Catholic Church in the U.S. was accused of being "primarily a white racist institution" serving white society. Blacks were no longer looking to the Catholic Church with hope, the caucus said, in describing the church's "extremely weak position" in the black communities.

The percentage of black priests among the American Catholic clergy is infinitesimally small—167 out of 60,000, according to an early 1969 figure.[7] Blacks comprise some five per cent of the more than 47 million Catholics. By and large, the National Conference of Catholic Bishops responded favorably to the black demands for black priest recruitment, greater black decision-making power, training for white priests intending to serve black parishioners, a black-directed department within the bishops' conference and diocesan funding for black leadership training.

A black vicar for Harlem was named in New York, and the Archdiocese of Detroit, led by John Cardinal Dearden, president of the bishops' conference, did not lag at instigating compliances to promises. Successes were not automatic in all areas of high black Catholic concentration. Father Rollins Lambert and Father George Clements, both leaders in the Black Clergy Caucus, found themselves in a running battle with John Cardinal Cody of Chicago, essentially over efforts to get black priests appointed to pastorates. Some success was recorded in the Summer, 1969. A lay group, United Black Catholics, joined an interracial priest organization in Newark, N.J., in charging Archbishop Thomas A. Boland with showing little evidence of sincere understanding of black or urban problems. The laymen questioned archdiocesan expenditure in social service, asking: "Why does he (the archbishop) not ask the black community what facilities it feels are serving, rather than fund some establishments which need financial help because they do not in fact serve their community and the community refused to support an institution that stands as an insult to it?"

Nuns also adopted a caucus strategy. The first National Black Sisters' Conference met in Pittsburgh in August, 1968, bringing together 160 nuns from seventy-six religious communities in twenty-two states, the Virgin Islands and Uganda. A permanent conference was formed. Black power, not separatism, marked the meeting. Organizer Sister Martin de Porres Gray of the Sisters of Mercy, Pittsburgh, told an *Ebony* reporter that white sisters and church officials were "on the whole unfavorable" to the idea, "though many wished us well."[8] Six hundred letters were sent to mother generals in the nation, seeking support. Two hundred replies were received.

The nuns conference is more educational than political. Said Sister Martin de Porres: "The church is predominantly a white institution and it caters to white communities. Since white racism is behind the race problem, then we, as black religious women, have to help white clergy and our white sisters understand white racism so they, in turn, can teach their people the truth."

Black Catholic caucuses have not blackened U.S. Catholicism to any great degree, but they have blackened, thereby renewing, black Catholic priests and nuns. Worship in parishes, such as St. Dorothy's in Chicago and St. Thomas the Apostle in New York, has taken on distinct black overtones. Paintings and statues of black Christs and Madonnas have begun to abound. Despite Cardinal Cody's condemnation of African-style dance at a session of the Chicago Conference of Laymen, St. Dorothy's held a black unity Mass with African overtones in January 1969, widely publicized because of the animal-skin altar cloth and African vestments.

In the caucuses, the National Committee of Black Church-men and to a degree in the nuns' group, a fairly predictable pattern was followed in organizing: statement of the problem —white racism; a defense of the black position—black power with a theological undergirding; a list of grievances, goals and demands; and the occasional threat of separatism in favor of exclusively black churches.

A far cry from traditional church pronouncements are the black caucus statements dealing with life and death issues of the black community. Outside the church but within the black community, there is a radical force that will not let the inherited oppression continue. Maulana Karenga, of Los Angeles' militant US, criticized black churchmen at a national conference for letting themselves be made stooges of the white churches. Should tokenism continue in the white churches, this kind of criticism may lead to general rejection. Add also the voices of psychiatrists William H. Grier and Price M. Cobbs telling black and white how Christianity has incul-cated self-destructive guilt in blacks not long freed from a social condition in which disbelief of the white master was sin, heresy and crime.[9] Doctors Grier and Cobbs were re-ported working on a second book, *The Jesus Boy,* which would extend this theme.

Black caucuses have been successful in sensitizing many white churches to the lingering racism within their lives. The approach has seldom been "may I?" Few church conclaves, except the semi-annual meetings of the Catholic bishops, were free in 1968 and 1969 of black caucus activism. The Unitarian Universalist Association had the first black caucus, perhaps spurred by a widespread report that the Association realized a racial crisis was brewing in 1967 and set an emergency conference several months in the future. The 1968 Unitarian national meeting was healthily torn asunder by the caucus.

Other black groups followed, black power having received broad black clergy support in a July 31, 1966, advertisement in the *New York Times*. The United Methodist caucus has become most assertive, partly because of size and partly because of the excellent leadership of James Lawson, a Fellowship of Reconciliation worker, advocate of Martin Luther King, Jr.'s philosophy, and a wise head in dealing with racism. Lawson, a pastor in Memphis, was an early sit-in leader who stood at the center of the "Lawson affair" at the Vanderbilt University Divinity School, Nashville, in 1960. He was one of the first students to be expelled by a university administration—not the seminary—for advocating civil disobedience.

Coupled with the assassination of King and the Kerner Commission findings, blacks got some action from the supposedly renewing churches. Racial-urban priorities were voted, and staff and funds were, as they say, deployed. Black pressure had a role in putting through the multi-million dollar "development and reconciliation" funds churches approved in 1968. The good intention of such allocations could not be immediately actualized—the sums not being in hand —and when the Urban Coalition and Urban America assayed problems and progress a year after the Kerner report, not a mention of church contribution crept in. Notable, since white churchmen have bragged about their participation in the Urban Coalition.

More significant than playing gad-fly on lingeringly racist church rumps, the caucuses have unified the black churchmen in white institutions. Although these groups started with essentially denominational concerns, their common problems have brought about a new ecumenism. Metz Rollins, director of the National Committee of Black Churchmen, said:

"There's no room to be doing these thin?? along strictly denominational lines. The problems facing ᵢᵤack Churchmen
are so common that it doesn't make any difference who starts
a thing or where it comes from."[10] This form of unity will
mean that black churchmen will speak with added authority
and should prove to be far more effective than spokesmen for
traditional (or institutional) ecumenism when their attention
can be extended to religious questions beyond racism.

One other important effect of the individual black caucuses
coming together is that it will help bring hesitant black
churchmen into this revolution. Black leaders have expressed
concern over the reluctance of some blacks to affiliate with
their caucuses. The black sisters faced the same thing. Perhaps, when they see the church union of their black brothers
and sisters from across the religious spectrum, there will be
less concern for the "total church" and more for their black
community.

The All Black Churches

Any discussion of the totally black Protestant churches must
be limited at this stage. These contain the *real* black power
people, holding power within their own structures and not
about to give it up. All black churches are largely untouched
by the renewal movement that has moved through white Protestantism, and with today's enthusiasm for "soul" they may
feel vindicated. However, these churches are also the ac-
knowledged bastions of middle class Uncle Tomism. While
they may be "soul" in style, they are conservative in theology
and politics; they continue to call themselves "Negroes." In
many instances, their leaders opposed the Black Manifesto
and its spokesman, James Forman.

The presiding bishop of the African Methodist Episcopal

Church did announce a new thrust in March, 1969. He said his denomination was going to help President Nixon "unify" the nation. Joseph H. Jackson, president of the National Baptist Convention, U.S.A., Inc., so unilaterally put his denomination behind Nixon in the Presidential campaign of 1968 that he was publicly repudiated by a small number of clergy. The dissidents were the same persons who have unsuccessfully tried for years to vote Jackson out of power in the nation's third largest Protestant denomination. Said one of the non-Nixon men: "Jackson and his crowd are looking for pie in the sky, but I'm looking for something here and now."

The white establishment can rely on the all black churches to provide black churchmen when ecumenicity or civic necessity requires one. Because they have carried on the "soul" tradition, they are quite important to white denominations, for blacks in white churches tend to give up "black religion" and adopt the formalism and liberalism of their new church homes. (The Black Manifesto phenomenon reversed this pattern somewhat.)

With the return to "soul," new problems arise. Two different religious communities meet head-on, though undergirded by a common blackness. Much work must be done in the meaning of black community, sociology, history and theology. Black leaders are well aware of the urgency of the task. The present thrust of the National Committee of Black Churchmen is towards the theological elucidation of black power and the effect of white-dominated Christian education on black congregations. This study is leading to the development of a black curriculum that will take into account black experience. The story of the black struggle against oppression, the witness of the black church and the early black Christians and the possible dark skin of Jesus could bring pride and faith into the black child's life at an early age.

But like the rest of American society, the black denominations and the black congregations in so-called integrated
churches have a "generation gap" which raises problems for
church renewal. The Black Methodists for Church Renewal
caucus experienced a youth rebellion. Earnest A. Smith told
the 1969 annual meeting of this group that ". . . already the
generation gap is becoming more and more evident." And a
student from Atlanta cautioned that ". . . if the church is
going to be effective, it had better change. What's more, we
young people want to have a say-so in what the change is. . . .
The main reason we have not attempted a church takeover
or a sanctuary sit-in is because we have felt that the church
just ain't worth the bother. . . . The church should encourage
love and unity to be the new bylaws of the black community."

Recruitment of black youth for seminary training is an oft-
cited problem among white seminary deans. Archie Hargraves, of the Chicago Theological Seminary, believes theological students are available if the schools will go after them
and help them financially—given, of course, a curriculum and
atmosphere in which black can contribute new symbols and
concepts.[11] Hargraves, Vincent Harding, of Atlanta's Spelman
College, and Shelby Rooks, executive director of the Fund
for Theological Education, are black leaders stressing the
link between black church renewal and theological education
for the new black clergy. A white, academic bachelor of divinity or master of theology degree is no longer acceptable; more
is required, a fact dramatically underscored by a Spring, 1969'
lock-in of nineteen black students at the Colgate-Rochester
Theological School, Rochester, New York. After the murder
of King, the seminary set out to make itself more relevant to
blacks, but students found the changes inadequate. Among
the points won in the lock-in were more black trustees to
shape the programs, more black faculty to lead the curriculum

and a field work coordinator to seek suitable work-training opportunities.

A 1968 National Consultation on the Black Church was held in Boston and was attended by over 400 black churchmen. The emphasis was on education and scholarship in terms of the black experience. Rooks pointed out that the problems of obtaining viable black seminary education might ideally be solved by forming separate black institutions. Since inadequate funding makes the ideal impractical, Rooks added: "What this means in terms of strategy, then, is that the role of black men with regard to white theological schools is to keep working at the reformation of the theological education experience in order to force it to be inclusive of the black minority in its midst."[12]

Granted the enormous funding required for black churchmen to accomplish the goals set for themselves in renewing church and society, they will not accept resources from white churches which co-opt their integrity or plans. Black ecclesiology centers on self-affirmation and autonomy, which are not the same as separatism. Black Christians are increasingly determined that the white institutions shall not sap their vitality. They will share their dreams, accomplishments, hopes and faith but rightfully will not surrender their hard-won independence.

The white church's preoccupation with service is called into court by the decisions of the minorities to quit letting themselves be bought off with Thanksgiving baskets. Amazing as it is, church planning sessions on "race relations" continue to be held without a black face in the room.

Naturally, the church and ecumenical agencies want to obtain the services of blacks as staff personnel. "Does anybody know a good black administrator, journalist, organizer, librarian, secretary or switchboard operator?" The corridors

of ecclesiastical power bastions ring with the question. Open
hiring, sure, but integration means receiving as well as giving.
Church bureaus are excellent places to whitewash black people. For renewal to claim its name, some blackening is now in
order.

Black Homework and the Cleage Thesis

Inclusion of blacks in the predominantly white staff-struc-
tures of churches—local parishes or world headquarters—may
seem a matter of secondary importance. Actually, it has substantial proportions. Consider a non-church context as illus-
tration. A black owned and operated bank is established in a
ghetto. It exists to make money, yet it also aims at making
capital available to persons previously anathema to the downtown financial houses. Most employees are black, accepted
with minimal or no experience. Given a chance, the personnel learn fast. Six months later they are lured away by the
downtown banks which are on the lookout for "good black
people." The ghetto banks hire other untrained persons and
the cycle continues. But what happens to the black owned
financial installation? It will probably offer second-rate bank-
ing service because it cannot maintain a core of non-mobile
workers.

Something similar to this can happen to black Christianity
if its leaders are siphoned off by white institutions. For this
reason, several black church spokesmen have called for a
moratorium on proliferation of black personnel in the white
bureaucracies. The request is not for resegregation. Rather,
it is for serious homework, the same motivation causing
black power advocates to say black parents want their children
to have better educations than white families are satisfied to
have. Some chasms must be bridged, not to get to a lily-white

shore on the other side but to reach individual and group understanding of blackness in religion, culture, society and politics. Gilbert H. Caldwell put the point in religious terms:

. . . many of us who have served with the white church have discovered that the quietness, the apparent serenity, the orderliness of worship serve to cover up the spiritual emptiness, the selfishness and narrowness, the perpetuation of the status quo that unfortunately is part of the life-style of white church life.

Every black churchman, particularly those of us whose church life is nonblack, needs to develop a new appreciation for the expression of "soul" that has come out of the black church. Instead of rejecting and denouncing the nature of the black church we need to understand how God has used it to sustain a people, to help a people keep their sanity; and now in this day some of us feel God wants to use the church to empower black people and liberate white people.[13]

Albert B. Cleage of Detroit is one of the most homework conscious black churchmen attempting to renew his people, and ultimately the church, with a blackening interpretation of Christianity. He has tried, drawing upon both Old and New Testament sources, to demonstrate the blackness of Christ.[14] Some who hear and read Cleage query his exegesis. He counters with a question regarding the scholarship that has allowed a white Christ to evolve. Cleage's position may be overstated, but it is necessary to develop a black theology for the black churches out of the biblical and historical sources of the faith.

Jesus was, after all, neither a white Anglo-Saxon Protestant nor an Irish or Italian Catholic. The adaptiveness of both the "historical Jesus" and the "kerygmatic Christ" is well documented in history. Black Christians have as much right to look at Jesus through the glasses they choose as Bultmann had to look through existentialism, Adolf Harnack through classical Protestant liberalism, Pius XII through the dogma of the Immaculate Conception of Mary and Bishop Pike through flower-power. And anybody who looks at Jesus will use some set of glasses. The original is unavailable for direct study.

Central to Cleage's position is presentation of Jesus as political liberator. St. Paul's theology, with its emphasis on individual salvation, is rejected by the pastor of the Shrine of the Black Madonna (United Church of Christ), who wishes to instill the sense of "a people" among blacks and so to serve the black revolution.

The depth of the Cleage pro-black stance and his identification as clergyman was a new construct for a black leader, and it has been model-forming. Cleage puts an edge on church renewal and relevance which is missing among white churchmen. None of the early clerical leaders of the civil rights movement, especially not King, were as black as he. Most men of his brand of commitment to his people would traditionally be expected to eschew the church.

Overtones of the approach of Malcolm X are found in Cleage. The strengths and genius of Malcolm have only sketchily been disclosed, though some reasons for his appeal can be determined. He was a strong black man in a white society, a man who never lost touch with his people, and a man who has influenced the black movement inside and outside the church. Malcolm was of the streets where he grew up and came to know his people. A strategy for Christian mission in the ghetto could be lifted from his autobiography.

Malcolm had a "ghetto instinct," and insisted on the same for any black man who expects to be a contributive black leader. Unlike one black man of importance who berated the white church at a conference and then returned to his stylish home in a small, wealthy Eastern college town, the Black Muslim chief urged identification with the black masses.

Albert Cleage's tenacious affirmation of the Christian church put him in a different camp from Malcolm X. His "ghetto instinct" and his identification with the people of inner-city Detroit is similar. To be sure, he takes part in inter-racial church efforts, such as the Interreligious Foundation for Community Organization (IFCO). Cleage does not, how-ever, allow himself to be co-opted into gracing stylish white church tea parties.

Black parochialism is an apparent stage in the Cleage style. The ultimate goal is something else, a demonstration of re-lease to the captives, whites imprisoned in irrelevant estab-lishments, Americans shackled by false patriotism, mankind living in fear of its own power and "Christians" shut off from the gospel in racism.

Churchmen in black America have more experience in relying on God than their white brothers who have well-laid institutions for support. They want renewal not to help the church survive institutionally but to bring about a church which is alive. Black Christianity is church renewal's only hope. But black is no assurance that, once racism is destroyed, a mixed institution could not serve its own ends. Church re-newal would have to succeed before the thesis could be tested. The world may not last out the wait.

Notes

1 Gilbert H. Caldwell, "Black Folk in White Churches," *The Chris-tian Century,* (February 12, 1969), p. 211.

2 Douglas Johnson and Frank White, *Experimental Ministries Survey 1969* (National Council of Churches, 1969), p. 6.

3 *Ibid.*, p. 7.

4 Grant S. Shockley, "Ultimatum and Hope," *The Christian Century* (February 12, 1969), p. 217.

5 John C. Haughey, "Black Catholicism," *America* (March 22, 1969), p. 325.

6 Charles Spivey, "Commission on Religion and Race," *Church and Race Memo,* United Presbyterian Church (January 1969), p. 3.

7 Christopher S. Wren, "Black Power Shakes the White Church," *Look* (January 7, 1969), p. 85.

8 "An Awakening of Black Nun Power," *Ebony* (October, 1968), p. 48.

9 William H. Grier and Price M. Cobbs, *Black Rage* (New York: Basic Books, Inc.), pp. 196-197.

10 Metz Rollins, *Church and Race Memo, op. cit.,* p. 2.

11 J. Archie Hargraves, "Blackening Theological Education," *Christianity and Crisis* (April 14, 1969), pp. 93-98.

12 Shelby Rooks, *Today's Ministry,* A Report from Andover Newton (March, 1969), p. 7.

13 Caldwell, *op. cit.,* p. 210.

14 Albert Cleage, *The Black Messiah* (New York: Sheed and Ward, 1968).

PART THREE / *Going Toward*

8 / Where Are We Now?

And you shall know that I am the Lord, when I
open your graves, and raise you from your graves,
O my people (Ezek. 37:13).

A striking fact must be admitted as the end of the 1960's is reached: church renewal—and therefore the church—is troubled. John of Patmos' "doom of Babylon" (Revelation 18) crouches over the institutions which historically considered themselves at the "supper of the Lamb" (Revelation 19). Difficulties both with the extant church and with facing an age of ecclesiastical geriatrics can be seen in book titles and in statements of hierarchs and bureaucrats, Protestant and Catholic.

A moderate Protestant, David Poling, penned *The Last Days of the Church,*[1] and a liberal Catholic, Francois Houtart, has written *The Eleventh Hour.*[2] A few years earlier, question marks appeared on covers of renewal tomes, such as John Robinson's *The New Reformation?*;[3] now the very subject of Robinson's book gets the same punctuation in Richard McBrien's *Do We Need the Church?*[4] Some of this is gibberish, like McBrien saying "no" to a "Ptolemaic, pre-Einsteinian church," "yes" to a "post-Copernican, post-Einsteinian church,"[5] and ending up, where he was sure to, with a confession about the Spirit being effective enough to keep the church from being destroyed by distraught Christians. But these titles are not minus a point. The "lover's quarrel" syndrome is uneasy.

Pope Paul's dramatic Easter 1969 plea to *clerical* "defectors" to stop crucifying the church is example of the anguish and frustration. The papal appeal confessed that Rome finds defection and dissent among clergy, the vessels of church authority, more threatening than laywomen violating a ban on contraceptives. The church could survive with an unhappy laity, not with deordained priests.

Another indication, probably a minority opinion, of a fear of ecclesiastical epitaph-time is United Methodist Bishop Gerald Kennedy's opposition to the Consultation on Church Union. The bishop feels competition among churches is an important reason why the church in America has remained alive. He reckons that an enormous U.S. Protestant supershell would end up like the Church of Sweden, everybody belonging but nobody going. Survival trumpets loudly.

Despite accumulated wealth, church executives have announced across-the-board budget cuts for regional and national agencies because the percentage increase of new money is starting to dwindle. United Presbyterian belt-tightening was based on the claim of being hit by the largest pro-rated drop in giving since Depression days, and this while the gross national income was booming.

Little Concrete Data

Yet it is hard to assess clearly the meaning of what is happening. Book titles fall in a category other than sociological research. Little concrete data is available. Not much serious or concentrated study has been done in the whole area of the church and its social significance and growth. Much that is said must be personal judgment and general observation. Accordingly, a new aspect of the times is that several options for the church are available and openly touted. Less and less stress falls on *a* position as being *the* position. Renewal, reform and tradition are all offered; whether they are viable is another question. Supporters for each position can be found in almost any part of the religious establishment. And to these three can be added a fourth option—rebellion. Churchmen take your pick—"Back to the Latin or Bible," "grass roots church," *aggiornamento,* or the "underground church"!

One small but significant piece of research gives some clues about church renewal. A questionnaire was distributed in 1968 to over 350 "experimental ministries" by the Department of Church Renewal of the National Council of Churches. (Of more than coincidental significance is the fact that this department voted itself out of existence before the completion of the project.) The results make uncomfortable reading for the renewalist and the reformer and will undoubtedly elicit an "I told you so" from the traditionalist and the radical.

Many renewal experiments, the study claims, were tied to the racial situation in the U.S. Innovated liturgies, team ministries, youth centers and similar efforts were mostly located in the inner-city, now known as black turf. These efforts, well-intentioned as they may have been, were hit by the rising tide of black consciousness saying, "Whitey, go back to the suburbs and fix your own house." The study clearly shows that "starts" in experimental ministries peaked in 1966 and declined thereafter.

Another center of renewal attempts was the campus. Widely acclaimed Christian coffeehouses, so effectively pushed by the coffee industry, as well as experimental liturgies, art, dance, drama, community happenings, were all to be tools of

God's avant-garde, the campus clergy. Lines were formed outside seminary interviewing rooms for positions with Methodist Wesley Foundations, Presbyterian Westminster Houses
and their partners on the campus religious scene. And what
happened? The "black thing"—but probably more important,
The War! Vietnam became the issue, draining energy, crea-
tivity and relevance away from the campus religious centers.
Vietnam was "man's coming of age" and Bar Mitzvah rolled
into one for the college student. From this issue students' concerns "umbrellaed" over everything that affects them—nothing was sacrosanct. Not surprisingly, students have avoided
the church almost entirely, except where they have found it
an occasional ally against the war or the university establishment. Even the newly-born and widely heralded University Christian Movement fell victim to the fray. UCM could
not accomplish the renewal of the campus chapel, let alone
the whole university.

The NCC study documents a number of things that did
not happen in experimental ministries: involvement of the
laity, combatting white racism, development of radical new
structures, and new pedagogical styles. Commonly, new ministries were issue-centered, often built around some aspect of
the racial crisis, and were characterized by a deliberate absence of the traditionally religious—worship, nurture and
adult education. Secular agencies were the natural allies, and
the Great Society programs proved a ready outlet for the concerns and talents seeking expression. The report also points
to an unstudied factor crucial in the present discussion.

There is in this country and throughout the world a rapidly
growing phenomenon of noninstitutional religious communities,
mostly ad hoc, sometimes issue-centered, sometimes liturgically
centered, often a combination of both, which *could* prove to be

significant in terms of the future of religion in our society. Their future may well be determined by the direction in which the institutional church moves in the next ten years.[6]

These groups, wittingly or unwittingly, see renewal or reform of the church as exhausted option. Work to renew or reform present structures is to them a waste of time. What they crave is a new set of structures that will join with other forces involved in the humanizing and liberating processes in this world and thereby be true to the gospel. The Liturgical Conference has become supportive of such groups.

Some will see the proposal to set up new structures as synonymous with forming another church or denomination. In a way they are right. If what is meant is another group with a structural frame claiming Jesus of Nazareth as a source of its teaching and life-style, then it is another "denomination." Denomination-making is spiritually dangerous and organizationally heretical to ecumenists. "Authority crisis" is a term increasingly slipping through the teeth of Protestant ecumenical leaders. Perhaps they only want to be in fellowship with the Catholic prelates they seducingly flock around or to demonstrate brotherly burden-sharing with the Pope. But at a serious level, the bearers of unity's banner no more understand a movement unsuckled on Geneva milk than Pope Paul understood Charles Davis. The noninstitutional groups, identified by the NCC study, care not about unity for unity's sake. They will not fly that flag.

Church people have been so theologically indoctrinated to believe unity means a unity of structures, and so warned against by its articulate enemies, that few words have been raised among mainline liberal Christians against the unity-equals-merger thrust. Thus grandiose plans of union go blissfully along with negative voices raised only by the conservatives, the occasional sensitive or angry radical, and a few denominational romantics. The theological justification for merger and union has been lost in the pragmatic, programmatic bases for these unions. As the institutions and bureaucracies meet deepening financial difficulties, the pressures for merger will grow, not unlike a dying corporation's attempt to survive.

The NCC study makes some tentative conclusions relevant at this point. It notes the rise of an action ecumenism, a new emphasis on "attitudinal change or enlightenment" and a further shift toward new areas of social concern. "These are the threads on which to build a future. Perhaps the most important piece of the puzzle is the very incompleteness of the future."

The future is wide open, but the standardized ecumenists may not realize just how wide "open" can be. The presence of a variety of *established* faiths and denominations has increased in the public forum (recall, for example, the praying by five different religious representatives at the Nixon Inauguration), but institutionalizing ecumenism holds the heads of church as well as civic leaders. The young are not interested. An appropriate anthem at most National or World Council gatherings, and definitely in official Romedom, might be the folk song asking, "Where have all the young men gone?"

A new ecumenical movement has been born, one based on common worldly concerns, and with worship growing out of shared interests. A season for new and heady wine has come forth. Concern over container-skins, new or patched up, is lessening. (If Jesus had known how the wine and wineskin parable would be batted around today, he would never have spoken it.) The ecumenical movement as official, organized cooperation is finishing. So may be the need for the merger bit.

Patching up old wineskins is the undertaking of the Consultation on Church Union. With due respect to the enormous labors involved in that production, it will, if realized, amount to a conglomerate church—with crumbs (and Methodist chunks) mixed together. Reasonable theological sophistication will characterize it, but it will fall far short in terms of creating some totally new structure adapted to modern times. Unlike Vatican II, which had the support of many Catholics, the commitment and motivation of a community believing in the COCU quest is lacking.

Paul Lehmann, professor of theology at Union Theological Seminary, New York, has criticized COCU because it has been implemented to date by "executive initiatives . . . seeming to make the tempo of church union a major criterion of ecumenical activity . . . COCU seems more concerned with the church in the act of saving itself. . . ."[7] Lehmann's assessment is correct, while all the time the COCU pushers have told of the great grass roots surge inspiring them.

The days of one way or one wineskin are not yet, nor are they likely to be. The era of frank pluralism, without theological hangups about the biblical command of oneness, has arrived. Thus the renewalists who believe the church can be renewed from the parish up, or from the consultation down, will go their way with plenty of support. As was noted previously, the church is anything but dead in its institutional form; in fact, it has more life than a number of other institutions in American society. Stephen Rose, who at one time almost scuttled his own "grass roots renewal" thesis, argues strongly for the viability of renewing the local church. In an interview he said: "In order for the country to change, you had better look to the local congregations, the backbone of the church." Similarly, Harvey Cox, in an address to a group of seminarians, urged them to go into the local suburban parish because that is where the action is found. This fits in with Cox's urging the localizing of as much of American society as possible. There is no question that ideally the local church is well-placed for popular participation and control. This, however, has not been enough to produce results.

Joseph Mathews, of the Ecumenical Institute, makes much of the local parish, pointing to its centrality and renewability. Hopes, however, are not supported by the facts. Within the churches that have allowed, in any form, renewal and reformation, there is scant evidence of churches renewed. The numbers game, plus irrelevancy brought over into church renewal, and the statistical decline confirm its absence.

The exclusion of fundamentalist and conservative denominations at this point is deliberate. History will likely bring them to a more sophisticated revivalism (renewal?) based on a literal interpretation of Scripture and a belief that God will intervene to revitalize them. They will probably move from a theology of assurance to one of hope.

The search for life and excitement and a quest for relevance in the religious community points to a new phenomenon.

The Underground Church

Since the "God is dead" outing, little has proved of great journalistic interest, religiously speaking, apart from the "underground church." (There has been a slight excursion into the theology of hope and the renaissance of Norman Vincent Peale and Billy Graham as chaplains to the 37th President, and the Black Manifesto.) A significant difference stands between the "God is dead movement" and the "underground church." The former was a theological detour that proved a dead end. Few have tried to walk down Nietzsche's road again. The latter, however, is real and concrete and, while one may shudder at the name "underground church," its existence cannot be denied.

The so-called "underground church" is important because it is a highly visible group of Christians, with invisible grounding, who have in one way or another broken away from the established churches because they see present religious structures as unrenewable and irrelevant. In effect, the movement is reaction to renewal. Adherents judge the church from a deeply religious and socially-concerned stance. It is probably no accident that subterranean Christianity "emerged" as frustrations grew over the Vietnam War and civil rights and especially over the ineffectual stance of the church on these questions. The church was preoccupied with status and institution building; programmed renewal alone was permissible. Church agendas handle wars and injustice with statements.

Malcolm Boyd, the most verbal guru of the movement, was very accurate when he said:

'Renewal' has often seemed to be misinterpreted, perhaps deliberately, to render a false appearance of 'liberalism' as a means of avoiding downright radical change. One seldom hears this word in the movement of the Underground Church. The concept it incarnates has, to a considerable degree, been bypassed; one is now talking about structural change instead of superficial rearrangement. It is no longer a matter of deciding whether or not to sweep dirt underneath a rug, for many of the rugs have been taken up.[8]

In a conversation Boyd put it another way, even more directly. "I am not interested in renewal of the old, nor in tearing down the present structures. I want to work to build the new." The underground church may be the forerunner of the new, but it is still too early to judge. A leading Protestant thinker, J. C. Hoekendijk, believes the trend will increase: "There will be more people who cannot relate anymore with what is going on in the mainstream of the church life."[9]

It is no accident that Roman Catholics are the most active group in the underground church. Protestants do not have the same problems with authority and discipline and, therefore, can migrate into new structures of worship and community with less strain than Catholics. The Catholic's move is the more radical, for breaking with his Church, particularly for a priest or nun, creates the necessity to go "underground." Thus, Roman Catholics make the greatest contribution to the movement.

Pope John XXIII and Vatican II were unquestionably (and unwittingly) the forerunners of the movement. Pope John began to open the doors of renewal and Vatican II confirmed many of his hopes. However, before those doors were barely opened, forces of reaction tried to close them. It is doubtful, even if *aggiornamento* were given full rein, that the underground church could have been avoided, but the calcifying of renewal sped up the movement away from the established structures of Christianity.

Roman Catholic presence is felt in many of the small cells and communities that can be found in almost any city in the U.S. Their influence in the form of liturgy and celebration is easily recognizable, as are the many ex-priest and nun members. As one ex-nun in her mid-50's said, "We're recognizable by the fact that we are young beyond our time, and we have a lot of catching up to do." But it is not a Roman Catholic movement; it is a catholic movement, and this makes it excited and exciting. The members are deeply religious people who almost overnight have broken down old religious barriers. Many find the underground church to be part of the hope for the topside church.

Classification of the movement's forms in a traditional way is impossible and unnecessary. Within one city are found many groups with considerable diversity of structure, worship and emphasis. Usually there is little communication between groups. Nothing pulls them together save the fact that they are against organized Christianity as expressed in both the Protestant and Roman Catholic churches.

Some marks, however, are discernible in the underground church. First, it *is* a rebellious movement. Opposing rigid structures, it tries to move against the ecclesiastical stream. Second, it is ecumenical in the truest sense of the word. Included are every "shape and size" of Christian imaginable. Similarly, a non-Christian (and many groups include them) can feel more at home because there are no rules that exclude him, nor does the liturgy say, "You are not welcome here!" The world and the worldly are welcome. Nonetheless, it is religious and, as has often been pointed out, the Eucharist has become the center of the life of the underground community.

Third, there are no obvious rules—yet. The name of the game is change and movement both in religious and worldly setting. Noteworthy is a Boston conference held by some leaders in 1967. Nonorganization, the gathering was combination of old-fashioned mixer and idea market. A series of annual meetings was not planned, especially not after Malcolm Boyd and Mary Daly yelled at one another. Daly told Boyd he reminded her of Francis Cardinal Spellman, now the late archbishop of New York. Boyd likened Daly, women-liberating Boston College professor, to the Flying Nun.

Finally, and perhaps crucially, is the merger of worldly and religious concerns. As noted previously, in Protestant experimental ministries there is a marked emphasis on issues, but an absence of the radically religious.

The kiss of death for the underground church will come when the denominations start wanting to fund it, or the National Council of Churches plans a conference where undergrounders allow themselves to be exhibited as specimens. So far publicity has been confined to a book or two, plus the press, but more and more analysis will follow. Hopefully, analysis will not lead to paralysis. Hopefully again, the movement will resist the temptations of the secular media. It probably will not.

The underground church will continue to grow and to surface. It may be the wave of the future in its open rejection of denominational lines and its frank pluralism. It has ingredients lacking in so much of the organized church, verbal excitement and hope about achieving a better world.

There are obvious problems that will grow with the movement. People driven together out of common frustrations need a basis for community. So far there are only individual groups with few outside sources of discipline, authority and nurture, and this is the way it should be. But it is difficult to feed continually off oneself. Here is the very trap into which the aboveground church fell—ingrownness!

The power of the organized church will also claw at the underground. Emmaus House in New York, discussed earlier, was once a sterling example of the new movement and is still so considered by numerous friends and foes. Interestingly, Emmaus tried to disavow its underground heritage, partly because of an out-of-date *New Yorker* article and partly in an attempt to show that a church could be, in director David

Kirk's words, "ecumenical and experimental without being discontent and immature."[10]

If harbingers of the underground church are coming to view their own creation as immature, nothing has happened except a modern incident of what H. Richard Niebuhr described in *The Social Sources of Denominationalism*.[11] The splinter group gets older, electing respectability over liveliness.

Father Daniel Berrigan S.J., has rightly criticized the secretiveness of many of these new communities, sans Emmaus House. Part of the secretiveness is due to ecclesiastical nervousness. Some of it may simply be that groups are small, relatively insignificant in terms of members and influence, and uninterested in publicity. The term "underground" would be directed against this latter group, rather than used by it.

The underground church is a grass roots movement with no obvious structures, but what will provide impulses beyond the movement is the big question. There are signs of growing, codified sectarianism and a new "quasi secular orthodoxy." Importance for church renewal is not clear. Undoubtedly, it will siphon off creative talent and energy from the church, and it may provide an act of judgment necessary to bring the church to its knees in repentance or failure. But whatever happens, the underground is here now, scaring the holiness out of the institutions.

Attitudes toward the Church

What now characterizes attitudes toward the church? In most of the traditional religious circles, frustration and despair abound. It seems increasingly difficult to find viable ways of breaking out and bringing new life to the churches. The flow of priests, clergy, laity and money away from the institutions continues. Pope Paul's Easter plea followed the announcement that two of his bishops and a member of the Vatican family had left the priesthood to marry. In the same week the newsmaking Ivan Illich of Cuernavaca joined the laity. The Pope called the present situation "an abandonment of fidelity"; some would argue that it is the church caught up in self-preservation that has been unfaithful. The schisms in Roman Catholicism seem more dramatic because of its supposed unity; however, the situation is much the same in Protestantism.

Those moving more and more outside the traditional structures are those who previously championed and trusted renewal and reform. Rosemary Ruether claims, "large numbers of erstwhile reformers are becoming bored and are moving off to engage in what seems to be more promising pursuits. The entire renewal movement . . . appears in danger of dying on the vine. . . ."[12] She asks, like an increasing number of former renewalists, whether it is time to raze the "superstructure" and reinterpret the foundation itself.

Episcopal Bishop James A. Pike, granted his various psychic and psychedelic hangups, made some renewal-like contributions to the church. Four years after he stored his bishop's shingle, he turned in his membership card. Bishop Pike and friends continue religious interests through a "church alumni foundation,"[13] an apparently growing non-organization. He said he had lost any "believing hope" that the institutions could be renewed.

Ruether, Pike and Boyd were major spokesmen for renewal. The loss of these charismatic leaders—and they have been such despite flamboyant ways—is important, but what is more telling is the absence of new renewal thinkers in the church. Ten years back a great deal of attention was universally given to reform—among hierarchies, bureaucracies, ecumenical conferences and seminaries. Now, those earlier stirrings are being programmed and pamphletized rather than wider pioneering taking place. A sign was the focus—some said, "finally!"—on a "theology of renewal" at the World Council's Uppsala Assembly. The topic should have been called, since that was the treatment it got, "theology *for* renewal." Walter Rauschenbusch, the story goes, wrote his *Theology for the Social Gospel* after the movement's pinnacle was past. The World Council desires to prepare a "theology for renewal." Ah, the comfort of hindsight theologizing.

Renewal has lost its serious discussion based on front-probing biblical study, theology and sociology. Along with the study has gone strategizing and tactic sharpening. The 1967 National Council-called Conference on Church and Society in Detroit frumped out. Planners were hep on strategy but uninterested in worship or education. The conference went to the four winds. Consequently, no strategy for the church's involvement with society was produced.

Local clergymen or laymen who want an updated church are dependent on ideas less scrutinizingly prepared than the denominational "poop." They are not getting that help. Lacking "bridge discussion," bewilderment and frustration results from experimenting congregations. The church takes on the costumes of the status quo or of some totally new entity in a "brave new world" where most people have not moved.

Protestant leadership is not as harsh on the "deserters" as Pope Paul. Instead of retreating—the pontiff has returned to pre-Vatican II outlooks—the Protestants maintain hope for a renewed but recognizable church. Two leading critics of institutionalism have raised serious questions about taking

the familiar structures into the future. Peter Berger predicts
that the existing churches will end up as small groups by the
end of the century.[14] J. C. Hoekendijk thinks the mainstream
church will decline as the underground church grows, Christianity in the U.S. entering a diaspora stage. This, Hoekendijk argues, is what churches should now prepare for.[15] Institutional churches will not accept the Hoekendijk proposal. It
is too much like asking a man with no relatives to pay all his
bills before he sails on a leaky ship—depressing.

Much of the discussion of churchmen in the 1960's laced
renewal and reformation talk into structural considerations.
The preoccupation will continue in the 1970's. Implied is
that if only things were set up differently, the "church would
be the church." Maybe. Newer voices are wondering if
"church" may be the proper gospel vessel at all. Those who
view the church, renewed or unrenewed, as one of society's in-
dispensable bones are already reacting to rumors of church-
lessness by shoring up defenses. Rumors filter down that Mr.
So and So, a big layman in this or that denomination, thinks
things are getting out of hand. And when Mr. So and So
owns half of lower Manhattan, church decision-makers in a
certain uptown building are forced to listen. At least, they
will. The same applies in local congregations.

The claim of the new radicals is that the churches as institutional pieces do not take their Lord or their faith seriously,
so that all talk about structures or renewal is vanity. Without
fidelity, the radicals say, why bother to shape renewal programs. Radicals see the moment as a time to abandon the established for a new world of religion. Frontiersmen are given a
thought to take on the trip by Rosemary Ruether. Observing
that she may be too much of a historian to make a good radical,
she noted the "ambiguity and finitude of every historical

movement." Movement away from the organized church needs to be reminded of the dangers of totalitarian uppity-ness.

Institutional churches, whether they die or remain as program-sponsoring museum associations, must be willing to remember that God has more than once called his people forth, or sent them away, from the established. The call and the charge is to a *people*, not an institution. Where are we now? The church is trying to find out where and how it can live comfortably and assuredly. God's people may be someplace else entirely.

Notes

[1] David Poling, *The Last Days of the Church* (Garden City: Doubleday and Company, 1969).

[2] Francois Houtart, *The Eleventh Hour: Explosion of a Church* (New York: Sheed & Ward, 1968).

[3] J. A. T. Robinson, *The New Reformation?* (Philadelphia: The Westminster Press, 1965).

[4] Richard P. McBrien, *Do We Need the Church?* (New York: Harper & Row, 1969).

[5] *Ibid.*, p. 228.

[6] Douglas Johnson and Frank White, *Experimental Ministries Survey, 1969* (National Council of Churches, 1969), p. 2.

[7] Quoted in Stephen C. Rose, "Ecumenism in Limbo," *Christianity and Crisis* (April 28, 1969), p. 117.

[8] Malcolm Boyd, *The Underground Church* (New York: Sheed & Ward, 1968), p. 3.

[9] J. C. Hoekendijk, "What's Ahead for the Church?," *World Outlook* (April 1969), p. 9.

[10] Martin Marty, "Emmaus: A Venture in Community and Communication," *The National Catholic Reporter* (March 19, 1969), p. 10, quoting a letter from Kirk.

[11] Niebuhr saw "sect" moving toward identification as "church" with the natural process of birth and death, a second generation not being

as filled with fervor as founders. In a faster paced world, there is no reason to imagine that nature is the only change agent. H. Richard Niebuhr, *The Social Sources of Denominationalism* (New York: Henry Holt and Co., Inc., 1929). Paperback edition (New York: Meridian Books, 1957), *cf.*, pp. 17-21.

12 Rosemary Ruether, "New Wine, Maybe New Wineskins for the Church," *Christian Century* (April 2, 1969), p. 445.

13 James A. Pike, "Why I'm Leaving the Church," *Look* (April 29, 1969), p. 58.

14 Peter Berger, "What's Ahead for the Church?" *World Outlook* (April 1969), p. 9.

15 Hoekendijk, *op. cit.*

9 / God's People Are Where....

... then you shall know that I, the Lord, have spoken, and I have done it ... (Ezek. 37:14).

The foregoing chapters have dealt harshly with what a large segment of the religious community sees as the hope of the world, namely, the church, and it has dealt skeptically with what many churchmen see as the hope of the church, namely, renewal. Criticism of the church has been presupposition and side product more than thesis. Pinpointing the ills of the institutional church is more thoroughly accomplished by men like J. C. Hoekendijk, Hans Küng, Albert Outler and Leslie Dewart. Moreover, an expanding chorus is despairing of renewal as panacea for producing a relevant church, since the inherited institutions have co-opted inventiveness and are smothering it as they smilingly pretend nurture.

Renewalists who hack away at the institutions for pages and then prescribe cures or prolegomena for fitting church-change offer, at this point, a model of almost irrejectable enticement. Put bluntly, they spank and then sooth, partly because they want to say something positive as a concession to institutions which probably pay their salaries, and partly because anybody who takes the time to write about church or religion is not totally divorced from caring about one or both.

The spanking-soothing syndrome does its work "in the name of love," an undertaking not to be despised. It wants the "church to be the church." The time comes, however, when words must be spoken "for the sake of love," that is, so

that moves can be made away from a situation in which love-
lessness has the lover's mask, and moves can be taken toward
letting love make its own way. The Christian gospel seems to
support the latter.

To engage in this final chapter in model-sketching for
church revision, edification or destruction would be to fall
into the same trap which snared and irreparably damaged
aggiornamento. It would be to let the inherited institutions
predetermine response to the Good News. At the risk of ending up as cynicism's handmaiden, no crescendo toward mas-
terful mission for God's holy army will be fiddled here. The
Shalom group in the Netherlands was reported to have based
a mock U.S. Presidential election in 1968 on the claim that
"the U.S. Presidency is too important to be left to the Americans." Likewise, religion is too important to be left any
longer to the churches. Hoekendijk is right when he says denominations should not be fought, "because we only sanction
them by fighting them, but we should bypass them somehow."[1]

Only a fool would say that all of God's "real" people have
left the churches. Bishop Pike's "church alumni foundation"
and the underground church have authentic places. Yet many
there are who cannot play house with Pike and who are
turned off by the romanticized, ad hoc revolutionism of the
underground. On the other hand, the institutional churches
are loth to give up insistences that they alone mediate God's
grace and love. Despite fresher winds in cathedrals, convention halls and congregations, the church would have members
and the world believe it can fashion and furnish meaning for
and interpretation of life if the church is but supported. Such
assertion is non-self-evident, not even when the church runs
insights from scientists, artists, political theorists or philos-
ophers through its mill. Certain illumination comes with the

realization that poets have always been more perceptive than
theologians (to wit: W. H. Auden's Oratorio *For the Time
Being* contains most of the nuances of meaningfulness found
in Karl Barth's multi-volume *Church Dogmatics*). And it does
poetry no good to be surrounded by jargonese prose.

As mother of the "queen of the sciences," the church has
assumed the right to usurp, excerpt and twist anything its eye
falls upon. This heritage partly explains why the institutional
church found it so easy to seize an updating spirit and saddle
it with the church's programs.

Expending effort on strategies to destroy the institutional
church would be still less contributive than drawing up "next
step" renewal proposals. People who want a conservative, or
stodgy, or ecumenical, or underground or renewing church
have a democratic right to find one. Whether the church has
a God-given right to be any of these names is another matter.
The decent thing for church institutions would be to die.
Colin Morris, former president of the United Church of Zambia and a British Methodist by lineage, has piercingly described the reluctance of the church to follow its Lord into
death. He spoke in the context of the need of someone or
some group to give a damn about the starving of the earth.
The Christian gospel is broader than the providing of chew-
able food, yet Morris' point stands:

Little men with shrunken bellies call the Church's bluff. They
challenge her to put her immortality to the test for they are the
visible tip of a vast iceberg of human need. All around is a great
sea of outstretched hands and open mouths that would devour
all the Church's wealth and time and love. To answer that challenge seriously must spell the death of the institutional Church.
She would die for lack of funds to pay her way, shortage of the
manpower necessary to maintain even a skeleton administration

and wilful neglect of her property, most of which she would forfeit anyway when the mortgage became due.

But we brush the cup aside. We don't die. It is the little man who dies instead. And so we lose the chance to discover the answer to the only ecclesiastical question that matters: if the Church dies, shall she rise again, and in what form?[2]

The institutional church will not die in this sense, for the church does not trust God or man. It is precious in its own sight.

A time has come to stop asking the church to be the church. Let its bones rattle as they will. Someday the church as a whole may be alive with faith. At the present, individuals and groups wanting to be Christ-bearing and Christ-receiving may have a more viable and responsible choice than attempting to renew the church's structure and thinking: to select a needed, humanizing endeavor and say, with Colin Morris, "include me out!"[3] to the other heralded ecclesiastical preoccupations, whether they be interreligious diplomacy or bishop-baiting.

This is not the same as dropping out of the church with a curse upon the lips. It is affirmation of human selfhood before God and can have memories, dreams and hopes. For many agonized minds who feel compelled to push renewal when hope is gone, a church-non-church attitude would be the honest course. A church-non-church stance requires rather dramatic shifts away from the renewalist approach of updating organizations and unifying dominions.

Seizing Gospel Initiative

One shift is toward a refusal to allow the institutional churches total right to determine what the Christian gospel is or how its mission should be shaped. To grant the primacy

of the church in initiating gospel leads to situations like that
(for Catholics in this case) described by Michael Novak: "In
our day, an impersonal, notional system has replaced personal
belief as the primary fact in the consciousness of Catholics.
Ask a Catholic what his faith is, and he replies with the words
of the catechism. Ask him what he believes, and he won't
tell you unless he trusts you. He may even be afraid to admit
his beliefs to himself, lest they reveal him as a 'heretic.' "[4]
Novak wrote the paragraph in 1964, and it might be argued
that things have changed since Vatican II. The most significant change has been the willingness of more Catholics to ask
themselves what they believe, not the willingness of the
church to relax heresy classifications. The growing number
of defectors indicates readiness to live outside the catechism,
perhaps even in "heresy," for the sake of a faith less defensive
and rigid than the technically renewing church.

Dogmatism, of course, is not quite as insisted upon in Protestantism, but the institutions are no less convinced than
Rome that they hold the keys to the kingdom. Protestantism,
however, is more dependent on supportive members than is
Rome and will be more threatened by a less formalized style
of religion. Membership declines terrify Protestant denominations. There are churches which begrudgingly remove a
statistic which numbers not a living soul. Protestants of the
ecumenical variety are currently generating considerable
energy attempting to keep up with the splendor of Rome,
now that leaders have been inside the papal chamber and
have seen how nice power is. Never mind that the dainty
audience conversation sounds like a five-year-old leading a
group of three-year-olds in a game of "polite pollyanna."
Protestants will cry loudly should significant percentages of
nominal or active members follow Morris' "include me out!"
pathway.

Recognizing Pluralism

Pluralism—religious, cultural, social and political—is frequently mentioned but infrequently recognized in church circles. Controlling churchmen often act as though the future shall be filled with "the good old days when there was no question of the primary importance of religion and religious commitment and of the duty of the state to concede this primary role."[5]

In all spheres of life, pluralism is neither fad nor stage. It is major reality, to be recognized in religion to a greater degree than having all major faiths in the U.S. present for prayer at the Presidential inauguration. Pluralism, more than secularism or technology, is the stuff the modern world is made of.

The church-non-church man must shift away from thinking the current era of rampant discontinuities is going to pass away. Theologians and church spokesmen have become fond of pedagogically pointing out the transitional nature of the last third of the 20th century. They rejoice or weep, depending on their philosophical roots or the effect of change on specific entities or ideas dear to them. Churchly harking of transition strongly implies that goal-making about where the church should be, once stability is regained, is the proper occupation during a time of flux. Church renewal developed as a kind of guide through the maze on the cutting edge of the transitory present. That renewal became the crutch to keep the institutions hobbling is more a violation than the intention of renewal's original purpose.

Church renewal/reform assumes arrival at a juncture where foundation-shaking ceases, problems are resolved and the fulfilling of goals commences. Attainment through transition is the very definition of renewal as its purest self. This is why the black churchmen are the only genuine renewalists in the U.S. They must break down barriers, overcome stereotypes, build a strong house of black identity and love those they have had to fight.

The aims of the white renewal vendor, once transition is behind, are less clear, simply because renewal energy has been fed into dynamos lighting the institutions. The collection of renewal jingles uncased at conferences is the most hauled about evidence of planning ahead.

As the verbal barter continues, and as the port at the other side of transition's ocean looks as far away today as it did a decade ago, wistfulness for renewedness becomes a ghoulish myth. Religious publications have played fascinating games speculating on church and society in the 21st century, but projections to a time when relevance is operationally ensconced lack reality.

The transitory nature of society and religion reaches no point where renewalist or survivalist can look back and say, "we made it." Preservers of the institutional church must continue their beam-hewing until doomsday, church unifiers must continue patching up differences until Gabriel blows his horn, and new structure seekers will continue to find the new growing old until the sun dies.

A church-non-church stance can shift away from nostalgia about the past or future. (Yes, nostalgia about the future is possible. It is worrying today about the depression one will feel next year when church contributions go down.) To be church-non-church means to be happily pluralistic; secular, religious, citizen, friend, servant, protester, commender, all without worrying about a church institution's health. In the

U.S. it is to know with Sidney Mead that: " ' The church' is not an aspect of the American's experienced order. Rather it exists as an abstract concept, a figure of speech, a theological assertion, pointing beyond the actual and confusing diversity of sects to the pious faith that each is a part of the unbroken body of Christ."[6] And it is to know that without being too pious!

Living in Exile

The church-non-church attitude, committed to a human need with a Jesus-like compassion and anger, must be willing to live in exile, exile imposed by some unit in the pluralistic world, or exile from the church.

Of all the biblical material, the portion speaking most directly to the contemporary religious situation is the Old Testament prophetic literature. The New Testament provides ideas about the inclusiveness of ministry and, obviously, bears written testimony to belief that God has linked his compassionate self to humanity. The church which produced and preserved the New Testament may have been too young to offer typologies to the modern era. Today's is the "ancient church." Even the contemporary sects bear little resemblance to the "primitive church" of the Apostles.

Though farther away in chronology, the prophetic era in Hebrew history bore the marks of agedness. Religiously, the basic characteristic of the society identified by the prophets was "apostasy," also commonly identified in the present world. Who the 20th century apostates are is not easily determined, some reserving the title for the unchurched and others giving it to recalcitrant, slovenly churchmen. Clue to who gets the shoe may be found in the specifics condemned by Amos, Hosea, Micah, Isaiah, Jeremiah and Ezekiel: injustice, hypocrisy, vanity, idolatory, deceit, buck-passing and foreign diplomacy (read Isaiah if the last is doubted).

Major prophetic literature, reflecting the period of eighth through the sixth centuries B.C., employs a number of specific terms for God's people in the midst of apostasy. One was the concept of the "despised and rejected" servant prominent in Isaiah 42:1-4; 49:1-6; 50:4-9; 52:13; 53:12. While the references are personal, the possibility that a group might be implied has not been totally ruled out. God is said to have bruised the servant (Isaiah 54:10), a poignant warning to a modern church which might wish to assume the role or to persons inclined to attribute their sufferings to persecution by the church! Also to be noted is that God is said to have led the servant to the slaughter, another point to be pondered by any who would serve, or seem to.

A second prophetic motif for the faithful was the remnant, appearing particularly in Isaiah 1-39. The remnant, down to God's man in Jerusalem, were those obedient to the covenant who would last out the travail of God's wrath against apostasy and be leavening agent in the salvation of the nation. The calling of the remnant was for faithfulness in crisis. In terms of the barren times upon which many of the churches in Europe have fallen, the remnant concept may have some application to the institutions of Christianity on the Eastern side of the Atlantic. Be they faithful or unfaithful, only a remnant is there. American churches might find it beneficial to begin learning from the European Christians—in free and communist-bloc lands—how celebration and service can continue in a minority status, that is, if predictions of declining active church participation are true.

Currently, the church in the U.S. is not remnant, statistically. Spiritually it may be rag-tag, unidentical with the remnant category. The church-non-church can shift from church as mammoth toward a remnant possibility. The goal would not be to renew structures but to maintain trust in the pervasiveness of God in the midst of a godless time, inside and outside the church. Isaiah knew a host of religious leaders who were not religious. The suggestion *is not* being made that any group appropriate for itself the remnant designation. That is called pride. The prophet never numbered off the faithful. He said a remnant of faithful men and women existed. A remnant is a matter of responsibility instead of publicity.

In the Hebrew prophetic literature, rejected servant and remnant are tied closely to life in exile, to dispersion of apostates and faithful disciples outside the homeland. When the armies of the East carried a large portion of the Jews of South Palestine to Babylon in the early sixth century, considerable expectation of an early return was expressed along with concern over how God's people functioned religiously outside their "promised land." Jeremiah wrote a straight-talking letter:

Build houses and live in them; plant gardens and eat their produce. Take wives and have sons and daughters; take wives for your sons, and give your daughters in marriage, that they may bear sons and daughters; multiply there, and do not decrease. But seek the welfare of the city where I have sent you into exile, and pray to the Lord on its behalf; for in its welfare you will find your welfare (Jer. 29:4-7).

If ever there was admonition for the people of God to live in the "secular city," this letter from Jeremiah is it. But again, the prophetic claim stresses God's action is causing the exile. Leave-taking on God's part is less implied than a prophetic expectation that the people can act with some maturity. A church-non-church stance affirming the appropriateness of exile is neither depressed nor nostalgic for home. The work is where the people are, in a pluralistic Babylon to receive from and serve.

Exile, it is true, carried for Jeremiah and the captured Jews a hope of return. Some did later go back to Palestine. Not all. The diaspora was not to be regathered, not even with the 1948 establishment of the new state of Israel. Jeremiah's letter has applied to the Jews through the centuries, their welfare standing in direct relation to the welfare of the city or state of residence. In sick societies, Jews have suffered.

The church-non-church man ready to live all his life in exile could suffer under the hand of a sick society or a sick church. He may not, and it is not important. He is where he has to be, out from under what Nels Ferré has called the church's protective umbrella.

In 1953, Ferré wrote a parable which is as modern for the renewal mess poised on the edge of the 1970's as when the church was first discovering renewal and a need for updating:

Once upon a time there were some people who lived under an Umbrella. The amusing thing about them was that they called themselves SUNWORSHIPPERS. Their former domicile was the House of Legality. . . . Then one day came a prophet with a new light on his face. He told them there was bright sunshine outside . . . and some listened and came out, at first with pain and then with unbelievable joy; and they would not again return under the Umbrella to find the Sun. But others preferred the way of faith in the Umbrella and heeded not his word. Instead they went on praising the Prophet of the Sun while living under the Umbrella. "After all," they said, "we know that we have been freed from the darkness of the House of Legality." And so they went on believing. . . .[7]

The church-non-church man is with his people, God's people with no shelter. Where in hell else should a Christian be?

Let the church renew itself, if it has room under the renewal umbrella. And someday when the money runs out, the dead can bury the dead.

Notes

[1] J. C. Hoekendijk, "What's Ahead for the Church?" *World Outlook* (April 1969), p. 9.

[2] Colin Morris, *Include Me Out!* (Nashville: Abingdon Press, 1968), pp. 70-71.

[3] *Ibid.,* p. 99.

[4] Michael Novak, *The Open Church* (New York: The Macmillan Company, 1964), p. 358.

[5] Sol Rabkin, "Heavenly Harmony, Civil Harmony and the Supreme Court," *Journal of Public Law* (February 1965), p. 420.

[6] Sidney Mead, "The Facts of Pluralism and the Persistence of Sectarianism," address at Union Theological Seminary, New York (November 12, 1967).

[7] Nels F. S. Ferré, *The Sun and the Umbrella* (New York: Harper & Row, 1953), pp. 13-17.

Bibliography

Articles

Caldwell, Gilbert H. "Black Folk in White Churches." *The Christian Century*, 12 February 1969, p. 209ff.

Callahan, Daniel. "The Renewal Mess." *Commonweal*, 3 March 1967, pp. 621-625.

Durkin, John and Mary. "Renew or Abandon." *New City*, July, 1968, pp. 19-22.

O'Dea, Thomas F. "Can Catholicism Make It?" *The Christian Century*, 26 February, 1969, pp. 283-287.

Haughey, John C. "Black Catholicism." *America*, 22 March 1969, p. 325.

Rose, Stephen C., "Ecumenism in Limbo." *Christianity and Crisis*, 28 April, 1969, pp. 113-118.

————, "The Ecumenical Institute: Ode to a Dying Church." *Christianity and Crisis*, 11 November, 1968, pp. 263-270.

Ruether, Rosemary. "A New Church?" *Commonweal*, 4 April 1969, pp. 64-66.

————. "New Wine, Maybe New Wineskins for the Church." *The Christian Century*, 2 April 1969, pp. 445-449.

Shockley, Grant S. "Ultimatum and Hope." *The Christian Century*, 12 February 1969, p. 217-219.

"Underground Theology." Special Issue of *Commonweal*, 31 May 1968.

Wagoner, Walter D. "Thoughts for Protestants to Be Static By." *The Christian Century*, 19 February 1969, pp. 249-251.

World Council of Churches. Addresses of Fourth Assembly, Uppsala, Sweden. *The Ecumenical Review*, October 1969.

Books

Abbott, Walter M., S.J., ed. *The Documents of Vatican II*. New York: The America Press, 1966.

Berger, Peter L. *A Rumor of Angels*. Garden City: Doubleday & Company, 1969.

Bianchi, Eugene. *Reconciliation: The Function of the Church*. New York: Sheed & Ward, 1969.

Boyd, Malcolm. *The Underground Church*. New York: Sheed & Ward, 1968.

Callahan, Daniel. *Honesty in the Church*. New York: Scribner, 1965.

Campbell, Will D. *Race and Renewal in the Church*. Philadelphia: The Westminster Press, 1962.

Clark, Edward M.; Malconson, William L.; and Molton, Warren., eds. *The Church Creative*. Nashville: Abingdon Press, 1967.

Clark, Henry, ed. *Manpower for Mission*. New Forms of the Church in Chicago. New York: Council Press, NCC, 1968.

Cleage, Albert. *The Black Messiah*. New York: Sheed & Ward, 1968.

Cox, Harvey. *The Secular City*. New York: The Macmillan Company, 1965.

Dewart, Leslie. *The Foundations of Belief*. New York: Herder & Herder, 1969.

Goodman, Grace Ann. *Rocking the Ark*. New York: Division of Evangelism, Board of National Missions, United Presbyterian Church, 1968.

Hadden, Jeffrey K. *The Gathering Storm in the Churches*. Garden City: Doubleday & Company, 1959.

Häring, Bernard. *New Horizons for the Church in the Modern World*. Notre Dame: Ave Maria Press, Inc., 1968.

Hoekendijk, J. C. *The Church Inside Out*. Translated by Isaac C. Rottenberg. Philadelphia: The Westminster Press, 1966.

Holmes, William A. *Tomorrow's Church: A Cosmopolitan Community.* Nashville: Abingdon Press, 1968.

Houtart, Francois. *The Eleventh Hour.* New York: Sheed & Ward, 1968.

King, Martin Luther, Jr. *Where Do We Go from Here: Chaos or Community.* New York: Harper & Row, 1967.

Küng, Hans. *The Church.* New York: Sheed & Ward, 1967.

————. *Truthfulness: The Future of the Church.* New York: Sheed & Ward, 1968.

Man's Disorder and God's Design: The Amsterdam Assembly Series. New York: Harper & Row, 1948.

Marty, Martin E. *The Search for a Usable Future.* New York: Harper & Row, 1969.

McBrien, Richard P. *Do We Need the Church?* New York: Harper & Row, 1969.

McMahon, Edwin M.; Campbell, Peter A. *The In-Between: Evolution in Christian Faith.* New York: Sheed & Ward, 1969.

Moltmann, Jürgen. *Theology of Hope.* Translated by James W. Leitch. New York: Harper & Row, 1967.

Morris, Colin. *Include Me Out!* Nashville: Abingdon Press, 1968.

Nolan, Richard T., ed. *The Diaconate Now.* Washington, D.C.: Corpus Books, 1968.

Novak, Michael. *The Open Church.* New York: The Macmillan Company, 1964.

O'Connor, Elizabeth. *Call to Commitment.* New York: Harper & Row, 1963.

————. *Journey Inward, Journey Outward.* New York: Harper & Row, 1968.

Paradise, Scott I. *Detroit Industrial Mission: A Personal Narrative.* New York: Harper & Row, 1968.

Pelikan, Jaroslav. *Spirit Versus Structure.* New York: Harper & Row, 1968.

Rahner, Karl. *The Christian of the Future.* Translated by W. J. O'Hara. New York: Herder & Herder, 1967.

Raines, Robert A. *New Life in the Church.* New York: Harper & Row, 1961.
———. *The Secular Congregation.* New York: Harper & Row, 1968.
Rose, Stephen C. *The Grass Roots Church: A Manifesto for Protestant Renewal.* New York: Holt, Rinehart & Winston, 1966.
Stringfellow, William. *My People is the Enemy.* New York: Holt, Rinehart & Winston, 1964.
Van de Pal, W. H. *The End of Conventional Christianity.* Westminster, Md.: Newman Press, 1968.
Visser 't Hooft, W. A. *The Renewal of the Church.* Philadelphia: The Westminster Press, 1957.
Von Geusau, Alting, L. G. M., et al. *Liturgy in Development.* Translated by H. J. J. Vaughan. Westminster, Md.: The Newman Press, 1966.
Winter, Gibson. *The Suburban Captivity of the Churches.* Garden City: Doubleday & Company, 1961.
Webber, George W. *God's Colony in Man's World.* Nashville: Abingdon Press, 1960.
———. *The Congregation in Mission.* Nashville: Abingdon Press, 1964.

Index

197